Restoring Playfulness

DIFFERENT APPROACHES TO ASSISTING CHILDREN WHO ARE PSYCHOLOGICALLY AFFECTED BY WAR OR DISPLACEMENT

by David Tolfree

RÄDDA BARNEN
S' ...E CHILDREN

RÄDDA BARNEN (Swedish Save the Children) works for
children and young people based on the UN Convention
on the Rights of the Child. We fight child abuse and exploitation
and work for the protection of children in Sweden and all over
the world. We provide assistance to these children and amass
experience through practical action. We influence public
opinion, values and attitudes in society through
information and education.

ISBN 91–88726–46–0
© 1996 Rädda Barnen and the author

Production management Jon Skurdal
Editing Kristina Holm
Language review Amy Brown
Graphic design Lisa Zachrisson, Neo Media

First edition: 1
Printed by Scandbook, Falun 1996

FROM THE UN CONVENTION ON THE RIGHTS
OF THE CHILD, ARTICLE 39.
"State parties shall take all appropriate measures
to promote physical and psychological recovery and
social re–integration of a child victim of...... armed conflicts.
Such recovery and re-integration shall take place in an
environment which fosters the health, self-respect
and dignity of the child"

ACKNOWLEDGEMENTS

This book is based primarily on the experience of seven programmes which have been either implemented or funded by Rädda Barnen. This rich experience owes much to the creativity and resourcefulness of the many people, too numerous to mention by name, who were involved at field level. Their significant contribution to this book is gratefully acknowledged.

Particular thanks are due to many people within Rädda Barnen who have offered a great deal of support and help in the writing of the book. I would particularly like to acknowledge the contribution of Birgitta Gälldin Åberg and Jon Skurdal whose support, humour and encouragement have made the task a most enjoyable experience.

Table of Contents

Preface

THE SAVE THE Children movement began in 1919 in response to the suffering experienced by many European children after the First World War and the Russian Revolution. Founded by Eglantyne Jebb, the movement started in Sweden, Australia and the United Kingdom, and was guided by a concern for the rights of children. Now, 75 years later, the problems posed by children whose lives have been torn apart by experiences of armed conflict and displacement have increased dramatically. The deliberate targeting of civilians (particularly women and children), the availability of weapons of mass destruction, and the huge scale of refugee movements have conspired to create a situation where children are more highly vulnerable, physically and psychologically, than in any previous period in history.

The UN Convention on the Rights of the Child now provides a universally accepted set of standards and principles for all those concerned with the rights and well-being of children, and particularly draws attention to the plight of children affected by war and by displacement. Responding to the needs of such children figures significantly in the priorities of Rädda Barnen (Swedish Save the Children). A great deal is now known about the psychological effects of conflict on children, and in Western countries, various therapeutic approaches have been developed. However, their relevance to other cultural contexts is now being questioned. Not enough work has been undertaken to develop practical approaches which suit the particular circumstances of the less developed countries of the South, in which the large majority of wars have taken place in recent decades.

This book provides a valuable collection of case studies of different programmes, all supported by Rädda Barnen, chosen to illustrate a wide diversity of approach. Although programmes in Sweden and the former Yugoslavia are includes, the principal focus is on the less developed countries. The early chapters attempt to identify and discuss the main issues to emerge from this rich accumulation of experience. While no claim is made to provide any simple answers to the many issues facing children caught up in armed conflict, this book does aim to raise some of the questions which need to be addressed in planning and implementing programmes designed to enhance the well-being of children, and a list of 14 guiding principles is proposed.

"Restoring Playfulness" is written in straightforward and non-technical language, and it is hoped that it will be widely read by people concerned with the well-being of children in situations of conflict. It will make a valuable contribution to the small but growing body of literature on this difficult subject.

Johan Stånggren
DIRECTOR INTERNATIONAL DEPT
SWEDISH SAVE THE CHILDREN

Lisa Hellström
DIRECTOR SWEDISH DEPT
SWEDISH SAVE THE CHILDREN

CHAPTER I
Introduction

CHILDREN AND THEIR families are affected by war in many different ways: increasingly civilians have been not only victims of war but deliberate targets. People suffer injuries from bullet wounds, bombs and landmines. Both adults and children experience various forms of torture, rape and other forms of humiliation, and children as well as adults become involved as perpetrators as well as victims of atrocities.

Wars have profound *indirect* effects on the lives of people: poverty and unemployment, the destruction of schools and hospitals, the burning of villages, a widespread sense of anxiety, despair and insecurity all have a pervasive effect on the lives of children. The need to escape, the process of fleeing and the consequent experiences of loss and of becoming "displaced persons" or "refugees" all bring with them a range of new threats and privations.

Recent years have seen a growing concern with the *psychological effects of war* on both adults and children. Though less visible than bullet wounds, the psychological effects can have a profound impact on people's lives. Children who witness killings, especially involving people close to them, who see houses being destroyed, who experience the fear of attack or bombardment, who become orphaned or separated from their families and loved ones, or who have to cope with the upheaval of seeking refuge away from their communities are likely to be affected in many different ways. These kind of experiences cause great distress and may have long–term effects on the child's sense of well–being. As well as possibly causing various kinds of physical symptoms, such experiences have a profound effect on the ways in which children perceive themselves and the world around them, on how they feel, how they behave and how they relate to other people.

In recent years, Rädda Barnen has become increasingly involved in working with children and families who have been affected by war and displacement in many different parts of the world. Some programmes are implemented by Rädda Barnen while others are operated by local organisations with funding provided by Rädda Barnen. They are very diverse in their approach, often reflecting local perceptions of problems, needs, priorities and methods rather than a clear articulation of Rädda Barnen's policies and approaches. While this has facilitated a process of innovation and experimentation which has resulted in the development of a rich accumulation of experience, it has also been recognised that this "bottom–up" approach has led to these different programmes operating in relative isolation from each other. The need was therefore identified for a project to bring together some of this experience in a way which both describes the different approaches taken, and which enables some of the lessons learned to be identified and analysed. This volume is the product of this project.

It was decided to adopt a case study approach, and seven programmes were chosen to illustrate as wide a diversity of approach as possible. Drawn from several continents, they illustrate work undertaken in a range of different contexts. Most are based in developing countries, but work in Sweden and the Federal Republic of Yugoslavia is also included. Several illustrate work with refugees and displaced people: one programme focuses on work in a post–conflict situation, and another looks at work in the context of ongoing township violence in South Africa during the Apartheid era. Some particularly emphasise work with unaccompanied children while others have a broader community focus. A wide range of different methodologies are used: from individual work with children to broad community organisation and development, from work to enhance parental competence to workshop groups.

Although the case studies were chosen for their diversity, they are not necessarily representative of the whole range of possible approaches. Rädda Barnen´s support of the project inevitably means

9

that some themes are particularly emphasised, while some potential approaches are not well illustrated: for example, children's rights is a theme in all the programmes, while more clinical approaches, in general, are under-represented.

Rädda Barnen, along with many other organisations, tends to use the term *"psycho-social"* as a shorthand way of describing the stresses affecting people, and of describing any programme which seeks to have an impact on people's overall sense of well-being. It is seen as preferable to the narrower term "psychological" and places emphasis not just on the individual's mental processes, but his/her interaction with other people as a vital aspect of well-being. It is acknowledged that some people find such terminology obscuring, and increasingly the term *"well-being"* is favoured by organisations wishing to avoid the more technical language associated with psychology and psychiatry. Both terms are used more or less interchangeably in this book. Both help to direct attention to the *totality* of people's experiences, and the importance of the *whole person as a thinking, feeling, acting and interacting being.*

The book is designed to be read by policy makers, practitioners and other people interested in this area of work but not necessarily coming from a social science background. Although programmes from Europe and Scandinavia are included, the book is addressed primarily to people interested in planning and implementing approaches which are relevant to the less developed countries of the south.

While the book may be read sequentially, some readers may choose to begin with the case studies, which are found in Part II while others may prefer to select particular themes and topics from Part l. Short illustrations derived from the case studies appear in boxes throughout the text of part l.

PART I
Key Themes and Issues

CHAPTER 2

Languages and Conceptual Frameworks

MUCH OF THE RESEARCH on the psychological effects of war and displacement have concentrated on the symptoms of Post Traumatic Stress Disorder (PTSD)[1] which many believe provides the most valid measure of stress. However, much of the research has been undertaken in Western societies, and assumptions and generalisations are sometimes made about the universality of PTSD symptoms. Even research which is conducted in less developed countries may use methodologies which fail to take account of cultural differences.

The formulation of PTSD as a diagnostic category is also based on a very individualistic view of mankind. Western psychiatry and psychology view the individual person as the basic unit of study, and tend to emphasise *intrapsychic* processes (i.e. within the human mind and personality) more than *interpersonal* processes (i.e. between people). But in other cultures, such an orientation may not be entirely appropriate. Unlike the typical Western society in which individuality is highly prized, many more traditional societies have a much more collectivist quality, with a valuing of such characteristics as co–operation, sharing and conformity. This is apparent both within the life of the family, and also within the wider community where, frequently, there is a much greater sense of communalism and collectivity.

In such societies, catastrophic events may be experienced in *shared rather than in individualistic terms* – a "we" rather than an "I" perception of events and experiences. Hence approaches which see the problem in individualistic terms may not only enhance the person's sense of vulnerability, but deny or ignore the collectivist resources which might be more appropriately utilised.

A recurring theme in these case studies is the need to understand how problems are perceived by the people themselves, and what resources the culture and the community already possess to respond to these problems. The task of the external agency can then be defined as one of supporting and enhancing these resources rather than replacing them with potentially inappropriate Western approaches to healing.

Moreover, people make sense of such experiences by reference to the *belief systems of their culture.* For example, a person who experiences nightmares and other symptoms which he perceives as being caused by the spirits of the dead is unlikely to benefit from an approach to healing which focuses on intra–psychic processes. The intervention of a traditional healer is more likely to be seen as appropriate. People also understand and make sense of their experience by reference to religious and political beliefs. Any form of intervention which assumes that people respond to traumatic events in universal ways ignores the *meaning* ascribed to events by the particular individual.

A further objection to the application of Western models of psychiatry and psychology to the developing world is that they frequently tend to see individual reactions to traumatic events in *isolation from the broader context* in which they occur. This is a recurring theme in this collection of case studies: the following example[2] particularly illustrates this:

BOX I: THE EFFECTS OF WAR IN WIDER CONTEXT

In its work in El Salvador, the NGO Acisam found that people's reactions to their specific experiences of the war were inextricably mixed up with their reactions to the post–war situation. A profound sense of disappointment with the results of the peace accord, a sense of failure that people had suffered so much to achieve so little, and the continuing problems of poverty and disadvantage compounded the problems of those who had experienced violence, torture, detention, loss, and family and community disruption. In their work they felt that they must attempt to respond to the *totality* of people's experience, and consequently they progressed from a mainly *clinical* approach to a *preventive mental health* approach, and finally to one which emphasised mental health *promotion* in the context of *holistic community development*.

Similarly, in refugee camp situations, it is usually unhelpful to split off people's specific reactions to *previous* violent experiences from their *current* experience of being in a foreign country and facing the many constraints and privations imposed by refugee camp life, and their anxieties and uncertainties about the *future*. Forms of intervention are most likely to be experienced as appropriate if they focus on the totality of people's experience, not one small part of it.

In South Africa, the National Children and Violence Trust[3] found that it was impossible, and inappropriate, to address issues around political violence without considering the wider problems of violence within an inherently violent political system.

BOX 2: A CYCLIC PATTERN OF VIOLENCE

The NCVT found that the problems of township violence were inextricably mixed up with problems of family and marital violence. Moreover, both could be seen in part as a reflection of the violence inherent in the apartheid system which was characterised by widespread human rights violations, poverty, poor housing, unequal access to resources, injustice, the migratory labour system and so on. Hence political violence, township violence, marital and family violence and school–based violence were all seen as part of a cycle of violence that had developed.
The approach adopted by the NCVT was to enable local,

community–based networks to examine the various problems and manifestations of violence experienced within the particular neighbourhood, and then to devise appropriate strategies to respond to them.

Traumatic Events and Reactions to them

The literature tends to use terms such as "stress" and "trauma" in a very confusing way[4]. Trauma, for example, literally means "morbid condition of body produced by wound or external violence"[5], but is frequently used to describe the *event* or events which have a traumatic effect rather than the *effect* itself. Throughout this volume, words such as "trauma" and "stress" will be used in the strict sense of the person's reactions to events. The term "traumatic events" will be used to describe a wide range of situations that are *likely* to be experienced by people as having a traumatising effect, but without the implication that all such events will necessarily affect different people in the same way.

What generalised statements can be made about the effects of violence, separation, and upheaval which have characterised many conflicts in recent decades?

First, it needs to be emphasised that there is *no simple cause–and–effect relationship* between certain types of event and certain human responses (physical, psychological and social). The reactions to similar events by different individuals will vary according to a whole range of factors, which may include age and developmental stage, physical health, previous experience, personality characteristics, gender and so on, though the precise nature of the effects of such individual differences is not well understood.

Second, the *immediate social context* has an important bearing on how people react to stressful events. The adequacy and continuity of family support and nurture, the intactness of wider–family and community supports, the availability of social contacts (school, peer–group etc.) all have a significant impact on the individual's reactions to events. Ever since Anna Freud and Dorothy

Burlingham's study in post–war Britain, it has been widely believed that the greatest effect of war on children will be in situations where the war disrupts family life and causes separations[6]. It therefore follows that *unaccompanied children* are rightly identified as among the potentially most vulnerable members of any refugee community.

Finally, as already indicated, the *individual's perceptions and understanding of the events* will also be highly significant. Religious beliefs, political ideology, and the individual's own ability to make sense of his/her experiences will all be important in determining what impact those experiences have on the individual's sense of well–being. An adolescent with a powerful commitment to the armed struggle during the apartheid era in South Africa whose parents were murdered by the security forces would react quite differently from a child whose parents were suddenly killed by close neighbours in Bosnia.

These various factors serve to mediate between potentially stressful experiences and individual reactions to them. The concept of *resilience* develops the idea by examining the range of factors which enhance people's capacity to cope with traumatising experiences. This is discussed further below.

Having emphasised the importance of individual differences, it is nevertheless possible to identify some of the common distress signs among children, though it needs to be emphasised that these can vary greatly between different cultures:

BOX 3: COMMON DISTRESS SIGNS IN CHILDREN[7]

Thoughts and Feeling States	*Individual Behaviour*
• ashamed of being alive	• hyperactivity
• no wish to live	• nervous tics
• excessive guilt	• over–dependence
• inability to concentrate	• easily startled
• nightmares	• cries readily
• flashbacks	• withdrawal
• uncharacteristic fearfulness	• sleeping difficulties
• depression	• regressive behaviours

- prolonged sadness
- generalised anxiety
- panic attacks
- irritability
- apathy
- fear of separation

- thumb sucking
- loss of bladder control
- repetitively describing or re–enacting a sig–nificant event
- avoiding talking about a significant event
- inability to play or changes in play

Social Interchange
- social isolation and withdrawal
- increased aggression
- defiance and rebelliousness
- excessive clinging

Physiological Functioning
- headaches
- somatic complaints
- failure to thrive
- weight loss
- loss of appetite
- loss of energy

NB reactions will vary between different cultures.

Frameworks for Intervention

The case studies contained within this volume use widely different conceptual and theoretical frameworks to guide their work. What has emerged clearly from an analysis of this rich diversity of experience is that the *language and theoretical construction* used by different projects have an important bearing on the strategies being adopted. It has been particularly interesting to observe how some projects have evolved in their thinking, and in the process have had to change their theoretical formulations. For some, this has created something of a crisis of identity in the organisation involved, for example, Acisam (see Box 1 on page 13) in moving from a clinical to a mental health prevention model and finally to a more community–development approach. However, the capacity of an organisation to grow and change in its understanding of the problems it seeks to address should be seen as a sign of organisational maturity.

In attempting to explain the different language frameworks being used, it is important to re–emphasise from the outset that the intention is not to simplistically define different approaches as "good" or "bad". Rather the intention is to explain how there are different and quite valid ways of looking at the effects of traumatising experiences, and hence different ways of responding.

1. The Language of Health and Mental Health

As indicated in Box 3 above, many people experience somatic symptoms following traumatising experiences, and it is therefore not surprising to find that some people will seek medical help. Western psychologists would tend to see somatic symptoms as indicative of underlying psychological problems, but again this may be an imposition of Western ideas. Bracken and Giller[8] provide an interesting illustration of how women who had experienced rape during the civil war in Uganda often sought help for their *somatic complaints*. In a culture in which fertility and failure to conceive are seen as extremely important for women, they argue that the physical problems associated with rape should be seen as the way in which they *actually experienced their distress* and *not* as a secondary symptom of an underlying psychological problem.

It is clearly appropriate for medical practitioners to respond to referrals only in terms of physical symptoms, regardless of their cause, and to avoid dismissing these as "psychosomatic disorders". Medical approaches have an important part to play in responding to physical symptoms, and it is important that medical staff have a thorough understanding of psychological problems and issues in order to respond appropriately to referrals. But an overall strategy which responds only to such physical symptoms risks addressing only one small aspect of a much larger problem.

Medicalised views of human problems tend to concentrate on the individual, and on particular visible manifestations of stress, to the exclusion of the context. The limitations of an "individualised" conceptualisation of the effects of traumatic experience have already been highlighted. Moreover, the use of diagnostic terms such as "traumatised" or "mentally ill" may tend to reinforce labels which imply abnormality and sickness. Most clinical approaches carry connotations of illness and mental illness. Although some projects which use the terminology of "mental health" attempt to project a positive image of *health* rather than a negative image associated with *mental illness*, the fact remains that in most societies, mental health is equated with "crazy people", and the more positive connotations of mental (good) health are not very convincing to the lay person.

A further limitation of the utility of the language of mental health and mental illness is that many intervention strategies tend to isolate "traumatised" individuals from the large number of people who have faced similar experiences. This approach ignores the large numbers of people who, though not necessarily seriously impaired by their experiences, might nevertheless benefit from programmes designed to help their sense of well–being. Also, by focusing on problems, pathology or symptoms, an unintended consequence may be to highlight the individual's sense of sickness or abnormality rather than building on strengths and personal resources.

The approaches illustrated in this volume generally try to avoid such labels and potential stigmatisation by emphasising that people's reactions to traumatic events should be seen as *normal reactions to abnormal events* rather than pathological reactions to stress. In many cases, such programmes can embrace large segments of the community, or even the whole community. The advantages of such an approach are twofold: First, they can have an impact on all members of the community on the basis that "the problem" is a shared experience affecting everybody. Second, they may enable the traditions and strengths of the community and the culture to impact on the problem. Rädda Barnen's experience suggests that this is of profound importance.

Some individualised therapeutic approaches do make a conscious attempt to build on the strengths of the individual and to avoid stigmatisation as far as possible. But the reality is that most clinical approaches are still oriented towards illness and still tend to create helper–helped, doctor–patient dichotomies which tend to vest power in the professional, and to emphasise in people a perception of their having an illness or abnormality.

2. The Language of Child and Human Development

Some of the programmes illustrated in this volume are based on a conceptual framework derived from child and human development. The National Children and Violence Trust[9], for example, uses Erik Erikson's child development theory as its central framework.

This project envisages children's development as being threatened by the atmosphere and prevalence of violence which afflicted South Africa during the Apartheid era, and this approach is probably equally valid in other situations of conflict. Using key terms derived from Erikson's approach, the project emphasises the effects of conflict on the child's sense of *trust* – in the capacity of parents and family to protect and nurture, in the capacity of the community to provide certain resources, and in the society to prov- ide both protection and a sense of predictability. A second key term is *competence*: Conflict situations serve to inhibit the development of cognitive and social competence. Children develop competence through exploring their environment, through play and through experiences such as school and other community resources. Conflict may lead to an over–protection by parents, an inhibition of play, loss of schooling and other social resources. The development of a strong sense of personal *identity* is especially important during adolescence. Identity is the result of a confident belief in oneself, an understanding of one's place in society. Experiences of conflict may undermine self–confidence and self–esteem and may lead to uncertainties, especially if there are deep divisions of affiliation within the family and community. Insecurity, especially faced by refugees, and worries about the future may compound the identity problems facing young people. Finally, the term *meaning* is used to indicate the young person's framework of beliefs and values which are important in understanding and making sense of political changes and conflicts.

A different developmental approach is taken by Hi Neighbour[10], a small non–governmental organisation (NGO) which works with refugees in Collective Centres in the Federal Republic of Yugoslavia.

Their approach was based on observations of children's playing and drawing, which indicated that the war had a profound effect on children's lives, even those not directly involved in the war. The developmental psychologists who devised the programme conceived of war as impacting negatively on child development, and based on a Vygotskian perspective[11] they developed a workshop approach which provided opportunities for children, for adults, and for children and adults together, to interact in a way which promotes cognitive, social and emotional development.

While not all programmes necessarily base their work around an explicit child development framework, it is, perhaps, implicit in all programmes involving children affected by war and displacement that children's development has been adversely affected by their experiences. The work of Rädda Barnen's Standby Team[12] (which deploys Community Service Officers seconded to the United Nations High Commission for Refugees (UNHCR) in acute refugee emergency situations) is an example of a programme which seeks, in a wide variety of ways, to ensure that the developmental needs of all children are met, for example through the development of education and pre–school programmes, the identification of especially vulnerable groups, and the restoration of community structures and activities.

3. The Language of Prevention

Another framework which some programmes use is that of *prevention*. Preventative approaches are characterised by "an attempt to anticipate risk and put in place actions considered likely to reduce the likelihood of the onset of difficulties, rather than respond to needs only when such difficulties have clearly arisen"[13].

One example of an explicitly preventive approach is the Dance, Drama and Classical Music Workshops sponsored by Rädda Barnen's Swedish Department[14]. Based on the notion that all refugee children have had difficult experiences and that many also face current stresses in their lives, these workshops enable children to express themselves (mainly in non–verbal means), to work on areas of difficulty in their lives, and to learn to adapt to new situations.

Like the concept of child development, prevention is implicit in many of the case studies in this book: for example, the National Children and Violence Trust in South Africa uses a community network approach to identify and work on whatever aspects of violence are prevalent in the local community. This might include, for example, work in schools which has a preventive purpose. The aim of working with refugee women in Yemen[15] was to develop parental competence to care for children, which can also be seen as having a preventive purpose.

Two of the case studies adopt an explicit "mental health prevention" approach. The evolution of Acisam's approach has already been mentioned (see Box 1 on page 13): they now adopt an approach which emphasises a range of interventions designed to prevent mental ill–health and promote positive health within an overall community–development strategy.

A second example is the work undertaken with a large group of unaccompanied young refugees from South Sudan[16]:

BOX 4: A PREVENTIVE MENTAL HEALTH PROGRAMME

This programme comprises a wide range of approaches to respond to the unusual needs of an exceptionally large concentration of unaccompanied refugee children who have had repeated experiences of war, danger and displacement. As well as offering culturally–appropriate care arrangements, a range of activities are provided to enable all of these young people to discuss their experiences, express themselves, articulate their needs and problems and receive personal support, all in a manner which respects and builds on their traditional lifestyle and customs. Wherever possible, the approach avoids singling out children with "special needs", and a strong emphasis is placed on the need for young people to feel part of a supportive community.

One reservation about the language of prevention is that when the question is raised "What is it that is being prevented?" the answer tends to refer to pathology rather than a broader and more positive sense of well–being. The limitations of approaches based on "sickness" have already been discussed in this chapter. In contrast, the language of "resilience" tends to avoid such negative connotations of sickness and pathology.

4. The Language of Resilience

The research literature on resilience is founded on the observation that under traumatic or otherwise adverse circumstances, some children cope and develop relatively well, while others fail to do so. The term "resilience" has been used to describe the characteristics of those who fare relatively well – their personal attributes, quality of family life, social supports and so on. Literally, resilience means the capacity to recover one's shape after being stretched or stressed, or, more colloquially, the ability to "bounce back" after difficult experiences.

Research has shown that resilient children tend to have certain "protective factors" in their lives which serve to shield them from the worst effects of the stresses which confront them. These protective factors can be summarised as follows[17]:

BOX 5: PROTECTIVE FACTORS
- a *stable emotional relationship* with a parent or other care-giver
- *social support* within and beyond the family – e.g. relatives, neighbours, teachers, peers etc.
- an *educational climate* which is emotionally positive, open, guiding and norm–oriented
- *role models* which encourage constructive coping
- an appropriate *balance of social responsibilities and achievement demands* (e.g. as between domestic responsibilities and school work)

- *cognitive competence* – a reasonable level of intelligence, skills in communication and realistic planning etc.
- *a positive sense of self–esteem*, self confidence and self-control
- an *active coping style* rather than a passive approach
- a *sense of structure and meaning* in one's life, often informed by religious or political beliefs, a sense of coherence etc.

It will be immediately obvious that this list has a great deal in common with the Eriksson child development framework outlined above. Programmes designed to develop and promote protective factors such as these are likely not only to be offering a *preventive resource* for children and families, but also facilitating *recovery from traumatic experience*.

As a framework for intervention, the concept of resilience is useful on a number of levels: On a general level, it serves to direct attention to people's strengths rather than their weaknesses. More specifically, it underlines the need to identify and strengthen existing support networks within the community, both formal and informal. It may identify the need to direct attention particularly to those children for whom personal and social resources may be lacking. It may also help to identify existing resources which might be developed in a way that provides additional supports to children, for example in extending the role of teachers to provide a more personalised form of support, which is illustrated in the school depicted in one of the case studies in the present volume[18]. In this sense, intervention approaches will be similar or identical to those which might be labelled "preventative".

Resilience has been described as balance between, on the one hand, biological risk factors and stressful life events, and on the other, the presence of "protective factors" such as those outlined above. McCallin and Fozzard's[19] study highlighted the important role of mothers in mediating between children's stressful experiences and their sense of well–being, and the possibility of their parenting role being impeded by their own stresses. Taking a similar approach, the work illustrated in the case study on work with Somali Refugees in Yemen[20] attempted to promote resilience among children by developing parental competence by strengthening women's social networks and involving them actively in a range of community development activities.

Although the work with the large group of unaccompanied children in camps in Ethiopia and Kenya[21] (see Box 4 on page 22) did not draw explicitly on the concept of resilience, much of this work can be seen as enhancing children's resilience by developing a wide range of social supports based on traditional structures and practices.

5. The Language of Community Development

Several of the case studies in this book adopt a specifically community–development perspective. Although, once again, there is considerable overlap with the ideas of prevention, child development and resilience, it is possible to identify a number of particular factors which characterise a more community–oriented approach:

BOX 6: TYPICAL CHARACTERISTICS OF THE COMMUNITY DEVELOPMENT AP-PROACH

- Community development approaches tend to emphasise the need for *long term development* and not just the more immediate relief of suffering
- There is a strong emphasis on the importance of the *social context* in which people experience stress, and not just individual suffering
- They seek *community definitions of needs and priorities* rather than professional judgements about them
- The approach tends to see *traumatic experience as one among many aspects of stress* faced by people: Distressing experiences of violence may be compounded by current difficulties such as poverty, continuing fear, poor housing,

---

unemployment, lack of social resources and so on
- An emphasis is place both on the *collective nature of problems* and the need to promote *collective coping mechanisms*. It sees communities as resourceful and potentially powerful.
- Community–oriented programmes tend to focus on *common needs within the community* rather than the specific needs of individuals.

However, within a broad framework of community development, different programmes pursue quite diverse strategies. Some, for example, attempt to combine a continuing focus on individual needs with this broader perspective (for example, Acisam in El Salvador which deploys local–level volunteer promoters who nevertheless retain a role in working with individuals). Other projects focus entirely on empowering communities to identify and respond to their needs themselves: for example, the Standby Team deploys Community Services Officers, seconded to UNHCR as part of their emergency Teams. Their role is to facilitate the process of needs assessments, to help to set up community structures which will assume primary responsibility for community services, and to begin to develop and promote whatever pattern of community services suits the particular circumstances.

Some programmes which do not use the language of community development are, nevertheless, seeking to mobilise resources within the community to recognise and respond to the problems they are facing. Hi Neighbour is an example of this. Though the stated approach is to provide workshop groups in refugee Collective Centres based on a developmental psychology perspective, one aim is to impact on the whole refugee community by influencing the pattern of social interaction. This serves an significant *empowering* function which can lead to collective action by the refugees to improve their situation.

Conclusions

It will be clear from the discussion of different languages and conceptual frameworks that the categories identified above are by no means mutually exclusive and that there is a great deal of overlap between them. Programmes based on a child development framework, for example, can be operationalised within a community–development context and may have both preventive and curative functions. Some clinical approaches emphasise both social contexts and the individual's personal resources, while community–development oriented programmes may have a clinical component. One of the attractions of the "resilience" framework is that it leads to actions which potentially serve *both* preventative and curative/recovery functions, and almost by definition is based on understandings of child development. Moreover, when actions taken to promote resilience are based on the idea of strengthening the protective factors already existing within the community, there is a great deal of overlap with the language of community development. So to some extent, these different frameworks can be seen as conveying some similar ideas but with different emphases, and are based on different theoretical foundations.

What most of the approaches illustrated in this book attempt to do is to avoid singling out "traumatised" children and treating them in isolation from their context. It is not that it is "wrong" to define reactions to extreme stress in "illness" terms. Rather it may sometimes be more helpful to see those reactions as normal reactions to abnormal events, and to envisage appropriate responses not as singling the individual child out for treatment, but to work in a way that enhances his/her coping abilities within the social, economic and cultural context. Most of the programmes reviewed here attempt to develop the cognitive, social and emotional capacities of children, to work on people's strengths rather than their weaknesses and to develop their capacity to cope with life events.

But the programmes described set about achieving their objectives in quite different ways, variously focusing on individuals, on families, on groups or on whole communities. A distinctive aspect of the more community–oriented programmes is that they attempt to diffuse psychological understandings, raise awareness and seek to mobilise resources within the community to identify and to respond to problems experienced locally, usually by developing resources which exist within the culture and the community.

In concluding this chapter, three points need to be emphasised: First, programmes tend to reflect the theoretical or professional orientation of the people whose inspiration lies behind them. On the one hand, such orientation gives clarity of thinking and purpose. On the other hand, a particular orientation may inadvertently serve to limit the breadth of vision of the range of possible approaches. Some projects have seen this limitation and have responded to it: hence, for example, Acisam in El Salvador was able to evolve from a *mainly clinical approach* based on "mental health" conceptualisations, to a more *"preventive" approach* and finally seeing its "raison d'être" as *promoting* mental health through a range of community development activities – see Box 1 on page 13.

Second, what is appropriate in one situation may not be so in another. For example, the more community–development approaches will be extremely difficult to pursue in cultures in which the sense of community is not very strong (e.g. in Sweden and Yugoslavia), or where conflict or displacement has created such divisions and mistrust within communities that such an approach is extremely difficult. This may lead to a decision that more individual or group–oriented approaches are appropriate. In highlighting some of the disadvantages of more individualised, clinical approaches, the intention is not to criticise the validity of such approaches as such, but rather to question their relevance to social and cultural situations far removed from those in which such methods have been developed originally.

Finally, all programmes will benefit from viewing the needs of people affected by war and displacement in a *holistic perspective*. By considering the whole range of problems and needs in the context of both the internal and external resources available,we may avoid a convergent view which quickly "locks in" to one particular approach without first considering a range of options. Precisely what strategy is appropriate to a particular situation will depend on a broad view of the problems being experienced, as articulated by the people themselves within the particular local context, and the resources available. No one professional discipline can claim to "have the answers", and any programme will benefit from a multi–disciplinary perspective.

What this book hopes to achieve is to explore the diversity of approaches, to discuss some of the key issues emerging from this experience and hopefully to promote divergent and creative thinking and planning in this difficult area of work.

CHAPTER 3

The Importance of Understanding Cultural Traditions, Norms and Coping Mechanisms

AS ALREADY INDICATED, Western therapeutic methods tend to treat individuals as the unit of intervention and to emphasise the value of "talking through" difficult experiences and the direct expression of feelings about them. When applied to non–Western cultures, such approaches may ignore and over–ride existing capacities in both individuals and in communities. They may also prove to be damaging to people by contravening cultural norms, intensifying rather than reducing symptoms of stress, and ignoring the impact of present as well as past experiences.

This chapter seeks to amplify this argument and to emphasise strongly that any form of intervention must be based on a detailed understanding of the culture, and should seek to support and strengthen, and not undermine, existing traditions and practices which may broadly contribute to the healing processes and to encourage resilience within the community.

An analysis of this collection of case studies suggests that the following points are particularly important in ensuring that programmes are rooted in the local culture:

1. *"Communities are not empty terrains"*[22] but contain within them a wealth of formal and informal resources which can contribute richly to the processes of healing. The problem, of course, is that

many of these resources are invisible to the outsider.

2. *In some cultures, problems may be seen in collective rather than individual terms:* As already indicated (see page 12), western societies tend to place great emphasis on individuality, but in many more traditional societies, problems may be perceived in collective rather than individual terms. This partly reflects what Katz[23] describes as the "self–embedded–in–community" as the fundamental experience of self. This is an enormously important concept which is illustrated in a number of the case studies in this volume.

3. *Different cultures contain within them different rules which govern what can be discussed, and with whom.* In Rwanda, for example[24] people would only discuss personal and intimate issues with close members of their own family and friendship network. This means that the idea of providing help based on Western models of professional counselling is likely to be both inappropriate and insensitive.

4. *Different cultures have different norms regarding the expression of feelings:* Western approaches tend to emphasise the cathartic value of expressing feelings as well as talking through difficult and painful experiences, but in South Sudan, for example, it would be the cause of extreme embarrassment for boys and men to express their feelings of sadness and pain through crying. Although it was felt that they might benefit from discussion about traumatic experiences, in this culture discussions would centre on events rather than feelings – indeed the language has few words which describe feelings. On one occasion a well–known Western psychologist visited the Kakuma camp and, as a complete stranger, had the insensitivity to ask some children about their experiences and encouraged them to express their feelings. Some boys were moved to tears, but this contravention of a norm regarding the expression of feelings especially with a stranger – would be deeply embarrassing and potentially traumatising.

Another example of such cultural norms is given by Nicole Dagnino[25] who, referring to the Ixil of Guatemala, explains that "there are rules for expressing emotion, and that merely expressing emotions can be dangerous", and that "they believe.... that a child will be born misshapen if its mother expresses anger".

5. *Western approaches tend to be heavily reliant on communication through the medium of talking, but this is by no means characteristic of all societies*: The case study on Somali Refugees in Yemen[26], for example, offers a fascinating illustration of the way in which western "talking cures" may need to be modified to suit cultures where face–to–face discussion of difficult issues may not be appropriate.

BOX 7: AN APPROACH BASED ON
COLLECTIVE ACTION

In this refugee camp, Rädda Barnen intended to develop the role of teachers to offer assistance to children through the medium of group discussions and individual "supportive conversations". For various reasons the training modules planned to equip them with the necessary skills did not take place, which proved to be fortuitous in enabling them to develop their own models of help. The result was a conscious decision to respect the taboo regarding the open discussion of painful issues and the inappropriateness of "talking cures" in this society. Instead they developed a programme which emphasised the importance of daily structure in children's lives, opportunities for play, the involvement of parents and a range of activities which facilitate inter–personal communication and the expression of feelings in a culturally appropriate way. Underlining this whole ap-proach was the importance of a sense of *shared problems* which were being dealt with *by the community as a whole*.

---

6. *Approaches may need to be adapted in situations of continuing violence and stress*. Much of the research into the impact of traumatic experiences which led to the formulation of PTSD as a diagnostic category was based on stressful events which occurred in the past and which were of a relatively transitory nature. In this respect, the situation in many areas affected by conflict are quite different. In countries such as Lebanon, South Africa and Mozambique, the

conflict was an ever–present reality. A Palestinian mother is reported as saying "Let's talk about psychology when the war is over........ You, the Europeans can enjoy the luxury of analysing your feelings. We simply have to endure"[27].

This quotation highlights two important messages: First, it can be inappropriate, unhelpful and potentially damaging to people to destroy their psychological defences by expecting them to talk about their feelings. Second, it is unhelpful to respond to people's specific responses to war and violence in isolation from the other problems and stresses they are experiencing in their lives. This is particularly illustrated in the case study on Acisam in El Salvador[28] where it was found that the particular psychological effects of the war were inextricably mixed with people's disappointment with the peace accord and their continuing exposure to the problems of poverty, inequality and oppression (see Box 1 on page 13).

7. *It is important that existing traditions, resources and structures within the community are fully understood* if programmes are to build effectively on them. The case study on the the Unaccompanied Refugee Children from south Sudan illustrates this particularly well – see Box 8 on page 34.

The case studies on the Standby Team and Somali refugees in Yemen both highlight the importance of understanding the pattern of leadership within the respective refugee communities. The latter study is particularly interesting for its emphasis on the need to understand the informal, and to the outsider, largely invisible pattern of leadership among women before offering a programme which sought to mobilise, support and empower women as a means of strengthening their parental capacities.

On the other hand, it needs to be recognised that language (especially regarding abstract concepts) can be a serious barrier to the development of cultural understandings on the part of ex–patriate staff. The process can be time–consuming, and in emergency situations, the time required is not often available.

8. *People's reactions to stressful experiences are, to a great extent, influenced by their perception of the meaning of those events*

The literature places great emphasis on political ideology in helping people to make sense of their experiences, but religion and traditional beliefs also play an important part. This is of great significance and will be discussed more fully in chapter 3. The point to emphasise here is the need to understand the frameworks of traditional belief, religion, political affiliation, national identity etc. through which people understand and interpret events and experiences. Involving traditional healers, churches and other religions institutions can be an important part of a strategy which seeks to mobilise and enhance the effectiveness of existing healing and supportive networks.

Before concluding this chapter, an example derived from the case study on South Sudan, will illustrate how a programme can be based on a detailed understanding of the culture:

BOX 8: AN APPRACH ROOTED IN CULTURAL UNDERSTANDINGS

This exceptionally large concentration of unaccompanied refugee children ended up in a camp in Kenya after a series of exceptionally difficult experiences of war and repeated experiences of flight. Care arrangements were based on the tradition of group living in "cattle camps" and the acceptability of care provided by unrelated families. A range of activities facilitated the children's recovery from traumatic experiences in a way which respected culture and tradition. These activities included story–telling, composing poems, recounting and discussing dreams, traditional singing and dancing. The involvement of the whole community was significant in emphasising the importance of collectively coping with shared experiences. Despite the repeated experiences of danger, fear and flight, and the fact of separation from their families, the psycho–social health of these children remained remarkably good: only a tiny percentage were functionally impaired.

Recent years have seen a growing recognition of the need for this kind of approach which seeks to build on and support existing traditions and practices rather than replacing them with Western models which can be irrelevant, unhelpful or even damaging. Nevertheless there is still a drive to "export" Western therapeutic models which make no concession to local culture. As Gerard Salole[29] stated of refugee situations: "Rather than actually encourage people in what they are doing, we have tended to undermine and thwart them by bypassing them and setting up our own institutions".

Many agencies and writers are beginning to see the value of approaches which emphasise collective action and which build on traditional ways of coping, but frequently these are seen as supplementing rather than replacing Western therapeutic approaches. For example, Tortorici[30] clearly indicates the ambivalence which is often experienced in progressing from Western to more indiginous and community–based approaches: the therapeutic and collective approaches are both presented, but the relative value is, perhaps inadvertently, indicated in her comment that "I like to think of the collective aproach as the "back door" to mental health". Community activities, traditional forms of healing and various community–development activities are seen as valuable but not, it appears, central to her thinking.

Rädda Barnen's experience suggests that more community–based approaches, building on existing resources, traditions, skills, and coping mechanisms need to be seen as "the front door". It is only if there is a clear perception that existing mechanisms are not proving helpful to particular individuals that Western approaches, which emphasise "talking through" difficult experiences, should be used, and only if it is clear that particular individuals will actually benefit from them.

Used inappropriately, such approaches have the potential for making matters worse and for damaging vulnerable people further.

CHAPTER 4

The Role of Religion, Traditional Healing and Political Ideology

IN THE DISCUSSION of the concept of resilience in chapter 2, reference was made to the research literature which suggests that one important factor in more resilient people is the sense of structure and meaning in their lives, which is often informed by political ideology and religious belief. Most approaches to psychological healing offer ways of assisting individuals or groups of people in the process of enabling them to understand and make sense of difficult experiences, accept and "process" the feelings associated with them, and integrate these understandings into their view of themselves and their world. Sometimes referred to as "psychological resolu-tion", the process, however achieved, helps to restore a sense of well–being.

Western approaches to psychological healing place particular emphasis on counselling and other therapeutic techniques as a means of facilitating these processes, usually with individual "clients" or "patients". However, Rädda Barnen's experience is that there are many other ways of achieving this sense of "psychological resolution", and that the most appropriate methods will reflect the unique circumstances of each situation.

Much of the literature on the importance of ideology in people's coping with conflict situations emphasises political ideology, but two additional factors seem to be extremely important: First, in many traditional societies, people do not, as in Western societies, envisage body, mind and spirit as separate entities but rather as an undivided whole[31]. Indeed the spiritual dimension may be an all–pervasive aspect of everyday life. Moreover, as indicated in the previous chapter, the *self* is experienced not so much as a highly individual and autonomous entity, but as the "self–embedded–in–community"[32].

Second, religious beliefs can also be an important source of meaning, and religious observance can provide vitally important forms of expression of the feelings associated with traumatic experiences. Taken together, these two factors mean that people will develop understandings of traumatic events by reference to their set of beliefs, and that meaning will be attached to events not only as they are experienced by the individual, but as collective, community experiences.

The Role of Traditional Healing

Traditional healers may have a vital and effective role in healing the psychological wounds of war and conflict. Katz[33] offers the following definition of healing: "A process of transition towards greater meaning, balance, connectedness and wholeness, both within the individual and between individuals in their environment". In their excellent paper, Katz and Wexler[34] suggest that healing is not just a matter of curing sick people; rather it "involves central tasks of psychological development such as defining reality and making the meaning clear".

In her article on the role of traditional healing in Zimbabwe's war of liberation, Pamela Reynolds[35] described the role of traditional healers thus: "As the tailors and seamstresses, n'anga (traditional healers) were patching and darning the fabric of rural society as it set about restoring and reconstructing relations sorely strained by war". Her experience was that healers were sensitive to the effects of war on children, and in their treatments they displayed a care and concern for children and an understanding of their needs. Various rituals were used, for example for cleansing and purification, and in situations where problems were interpreted as being caused by spirit possession the healers could intervene in family groups to try to resolve the problem – for example if it were caused by an old quarrel.

The case study on the National Children and Violence Trust[36] in this present volume illustrates the value of psychologists working with traditional healers in South Africa. Based on the observation that many people still have faith and confidence in traditional forms of healing, the Trust's psychologists tried to adopt an attitude of respect rather than judgement towards them, and to seek to work in partnership with them. The case study provides an example of a traditional practice which was found to be effective in working with young people who had been the perpetrators of township violence.

Similarly, in their work with the unaccompanied refugee children from South Sudan[37], Rädda Barnen sought to use the knowledge and skills of the traditional healers in the Pignudo and Kakuma camps. This was a society in which, despite strong Christian beliefs, many events were understood by reference to spirits: death, for example might be looked upon as having to do with spiritual anger or disappointment.

The Role of Religion

During the Second World War, churches in Europe became unusually well–attended, people tending to turn to religion in times of crisis. But war and displacement can also serve both to weaken people's faith, and to disrupt religious institutions.

While undertaking the fieldwork for the case study on the work of the Standby Team, the writer interviewed a Rwandese refugee who movingly explained that although the majority of the refugees were Christian, "we have forgotten God because of the war ..... God has done bad things to us". Another young refugee, a devout Catholic explained how she would normally seek consolation for her own profound sense of loss (almost all of her family died in the massacres in Rwanda) from a priest, but the lack of priests in the camp was a great problem to her: without a priest she felt unable to pray.

Among international organisations there is sometimes a sensitivity about encouraging religious institutions in refugee camps, especially where religious divisions exist. But in the Karagwe District of Tanzania there were huge numbers of Rwandese refugees who had witnessed (and in many case had taken part in) the most terrible atrocities. Given that the majority were Christian, there was potentially a vital role for the churches in administering healing on a wide variety of levels: helping people to mourn even though no burial had been possible, supporting bereaved people, providing forgiveness for the committing of atrocities and conducting ceremonies of healing. Unfortunately the lack of priests in some camps meant that people were denied the vital role that the church could potentially play in healing the wounds of war. An additional problem was that some priests themselves had been involved in atrocities in Rwanda.

By way of contrast, the Case Studies on the Unaccompanied Minors of South Sudan, and that on the work of the National Children and Violence Trust offer examples of the role of religion in helping to mitigate the psychological effects of war. In the former, Christian worship provided a forum for the expression of emotion and for the offering of support and consolation. The case study on the NCVT highlights the role of some African churches in conducting large, community–based healing ceremonies.

Another example of the role of religion is provided by the case study in Yemen[38]: In this Islamic society, practices such as reading the Koran were found to be effective as a means of assisting children who were troubled by their experiences. Teachers, too, used such practices as a means of dealing with their own difficult experiences. Describing Buddhist societies, Garbarino et al[39] write that remembering and honouring the dead can "provide a useful sense of connection that can help comfort an orphaned child".

Political Ideology

It has long been recognised that both religious and political ideology can serve to protect people against the most severe consequences of stressful conditions. Bettelheim's[40] observations of people's reactions to life in Nazi concentration camps led him to acknowledge the importance of ideological commitment, and in particular, in his experience, ultra–religious beliefs and communist ideology.

Speaking of the situation in Central America, Jose–Luis Henriquez[41] suggests that child soldiers are better able to cope with the effects of war than child civilians who had witnessed the war because they can understand the war from an ideological point of view. On the other hand, they were ill–prepared for life after the end of conflict, having few skills apart from fighting.

However, as Garbarino[42] emphasises, "Ideology is a paradoxical resource. On the one hand, it bolsters and supports adults and thus increases their capacity to remain functional and accessible for children. On the other hand, it may prolong and intensify situations of conflict and in the long run increase the challenges to which children and parents must respond". This is probably most clearly illustrated in Palestine, where ideological commitment has, on the one hand, bound Palestinians together in a common cause, providing both support and a sense of solidarity which has had beneficial mental health effects. On the other hand, such a commitment has been, and to some extent continues to be a barrier to the creation of peace in the region.

The work of Acisam in El Salvador illustrates another facet of this paradoxical effect of ideology in situations of conflict.

BOX 9: THE EFFECTS OF IDEOLOGICAL COMMITMENT

Born in the years of the most extreme oppression in El Salvador, Acisam was closely associated with the various political groupings associated with the FMLN. It was their experience that people who were directly involved in the armed struggle generally coped better psychologically than the civilian population during the period of the conflict. They had a strong ideological commitment to the armed struggle, and they experienced a great sense of camaraderie

and support. But after the end of the war, the psychological effects were more apparent, and a particular factor
was the "military ethic" which dictated, for example, that
the showing of feelings is a sign of weakness.
Consequently, many of the combatants experienced
considerable difficulties after the end of the war, with the
phenomenon of "frozen grief" being frequently observed.
Because Acisam was clearly identified with particular
political groups, during the conflict it was possible for them
to gain the trust of communities supportive of the FLMN,
and hence to work effectively on the psychological issues
raised by the conflict. However, since the end of the war,
this political identification has limited the extent to which
they can gain the trust of communities which are more
heterogenous politically, and hence it has been difficult to
work towards community reconcilition.

Conclusions

People caught up in traumatic experiences such as conflict and displacement have a vital psychological need to understand and make
sense of their experiences using whatever frameworks of understanding they find helpful in their particular culture and situation. Religion, traditional beliefs and traditional forms of healing, and political ideology may all provide a sense of meaning and hence facilitate
the integration of difficult and painful experience into people's view
of themselves and their world. Any outside intervention needs to
take account of, and seek to support, those aspects of people's lives
which help to provide meaning.

This chapter is concluded with a reminder that adolescents,
already normally struggling with their emerging sense of personal
identity, may experience war and displacement as most disturbing to
their sense of well–being. Adolescents in conflict situations are
immersed in history–in–the–making, when the surrounding beliefs,
loyalties and ideologies are thrown into turmoil, and with them their
emerging sense of "who am I?" and "what do I stand for?". It is almost
impossible for young people to be neutral. They may be forced to

41

make ideological choices and identifications which they may not be developmentally ready for, and they may become actively involved in the conflict. The involvement of youth in the forefront of the armed struggle in South Africa is a clear example of this.

This is a difficult area for external agencies, particularly those wishing to maintain a neutral stance in both political and religious terms. The challenge is to help to provide ways in which people can make sense of their experiences, without the danger of encouraging extremist beliefs which may serve to prolong conflict.

CHAPTER 5

The Importance of Parenting

THE WORK OF Anna Freud in looking at the responses of children in England during the Second World War, and other studies during this period suggest that it is not so much the actual experience of war which affects children, but rather the degree of emotional upset displayed by parents and other adults in the child's life. As Freud and Burlingham[43] observed: "The war acquires comparatively little significance for children so long as it only threatens their lives, disturbs their material comfort or cuts their food rations. It becomes enormously significant the moment it breaks up family life and uproots the first emotional attachments of the child within the family group".

The family, in almost all societies, is the main source of protection and care for children, but the capacity of the family to exercise its responsibilities towards children may be impaired by their experience of conflict and their consequent sense of well-being. The practical and material problems which they may experience and the social support which they receive will be important in determining the extent to which parents (or other caregivers) will be able to provide sufficient nurture and support to their children. The ability of family members to understand and make sense of their experiences will also be important in determining their capacity to shield their children from the worst effects of conflict and displacement.

Two major issues emerge from the above: first, that supporting parents and enhancing their parental competence needs to be given high priority in refugee and conflict situations; and second that children who do not have families to support, nurture and protect them need to be given the most urgent priority. Each of these issues will now be considered in more detail.

Supporting and Enhancing Parental Competence

"The family, as the fundamental group of society and the natural environment for the growth and well–being of all its members and particularly children, should be afforded the necessary protection and assistance so that it can fully assume its responsibilities within the community" [44]

Writing of the situation of refugees in the Federal Republic of Yugoslavia, Nenad Rudic et al.[45] observe: "Their mothers watched television for hours, day after day, waited for the news from their homeland, and were concerned about their relatives. They were completely absorbed in feelings of sadness, so they were not able to recognise and respond to emotional needs of their children". In these Collective Centres, where meals were provided by staff, refugee women were denied many of their normal household and parenting roles. By contrast, in the more typical refugee camp situation in the developing world, women are usually faced with excessive demands on their time, and may lack the economic and social support if their husbands are not with them. In either case, however, the impact of their situation on their parenting capacity is obvious.

While the main emphasis in the literature is on the role of women, men are also affected by their experiences of exile, and their loss of status as a result of losing their economic providing role can also have a profound impact on the dynamics in the family. Often women and girls retain more of their traditional tasks which may enable them to cope more effectively than men and boys.

A picture of the impact of traumatic past experiences and current stresses affecting refugee women from Somalia in a refugee camp in Yemen is provided by a case study[46] contained in this volume:

BOX 10: PARENTAL CAPACITY AMONG SOMALI REFUGEE WOMEN IN YEMEN

A survey among refugee mothers in the camp, undertaken by Rädda Barnen, revealed that their sense of well–being was extremely poor. Half of the mothers interviewed expressed a high degree of psycho–somatic and emotional problems, and 85 per cent reported as daily experiencing various stress factors to an extreme degree. About 90 per cent of the mothers expressed feelings of helplessness about bringing up their children, yet a similar proportion con-sidered themselves to be the most important person in their child's life.

Following this survey, it was felt that the most appropriate means of enhancing mothers' parental competence would be by strengthening women's social networks and thereby increase their participation in the life of the community and give them a greater sense of control over their own lives.

In her excellent discussion of "Refugee Women and Family Life", Elizabeth Ferris[47] writes: "When the mother is able to fulfill her role, the difficulties of camp life are lessened for the child.... The mother can help interpret past traumatic events, help the child to under-stand what happened, and alleviate feelings of stress and guilt. But in order for this to occur, the mother must be physically and psychologically able to play this supportive role". The implications of this are that women need to be supported both as women and as mothers. They need to be seen both as potentially vulnerable and as highly resourceful. Programmes must not only be available but rele-vant to women's particular needs, and accessible to women who may have many demands on their time, including the care of young children.

A wide range of different approaches can have an impact on the

45

well–being of women: from appropriate and accessible health services to economic activities, from educational opportunities to cultural and recreational activities. While some programmes have specifically aimed at enhancing parental competence, for example Homecraft Groups[48], others attempt more generally to improve the quality of life and opportunities for the development of women.

Many approaches concentrate on the *empowerment* of women, in the belief that women are strong and resourceful but frequently lack the power to assume greater control over their lives – see Box 10 as an example. The work of the Standby Team in refugee emergencies places particular emphasis on the need, early on in refugee emergencies, to facilitate refugee leadership, including female representation on camp committees and to involve refugees, especially women, in assuming responsibility for identifying needs and determining how they should be met. The case study on the Work of the Standby Team in this volume[49] illustrates how such a strategy can be effective in enabling women to take the initiative to organise themselves, to set up women's groups and to take action on a self–help basis.

Sometimes, however, this conflicts with traditions of male dominance. In the Afghan refugee camps in Pakistan, for example, it was found that winning the confidence of men was required before effective work could be done with women[50].

The literature on resilience emphasises the importance of social networks in enhancing the resilience of children and parents. One serious consequence of becoming a refugee is that social networks are effectively destroyed, but in some instances it has been possible to relocate refugees within their original community groupings, with obvious benefits in restoring existing supportive networks. An example of this is given in the case study on the work of the Standby Team[51].

In response to the lack of supportive networks in refugee situations, Alistair Ager[52] offers a useful four–fold prescripition:

• Avoid disruption of existing social networks in programme implementation

- Facilitate "reconnection" of previous networks
- Prompt new, adaptive networks
- Avoid imposition of alien structures

This kind of networking approach is likely to prove to be an effective and a highly cost–effective way of mobilising the personal resources of refugees, especially women. It is especially important to find ways of building on their strengths and not to inadvertently remove power and skills from refugees by imposing unfamiliar approaches.

The literature on children affected by war is often found to place emphasis on this important issue of supporting parents and enhancing parental competence. However, the case studies in the present volume provide some interesting examples of the *dynamic* relationship between parents' needs and resources and children's needs and resources. The experience of Hi Neighbour[53] in the Federal Republic of Yugoslavia provides a particularly interesting example:

BOX II: CHILDREN PROMOTING CHANGE IN ADULTS

In the Collective Centres, Hi Neighbour frequently found that parents were unable to meet the emotional needs of their children, and moreover that sometimes children sought to "protect" their parents from emotional expression because they perceived them to be vulnerable. By involving both children and adults in workshop groups, based on a developmental psychology approach, Hi Neighbour found that even young children could effect change in their parents by encouraging spontaneity, playfulness and the expression of feelings.

Another example of reaching adults through young people comes from the case study on the work of Acisam in El Salvador[54]:

The approaches described in this chapter which aim to find various
ways of supporting parents are of equal relevance to other adults
(and older brothers and sisters) who have assumed the responsibility
of caring for children who have become separated from their
families. Indeed, because of the additional responsibilities such
people have taken on, they may especially need additional support.
The care of unaccompanied children is the subject of the next part
of this chapter.

Care for Unaccompanied Children

*"A child temporarily or permanently deprived of his or her family
environment ... shall be entitled to special protection and assistance ..."*[55]

The introduction to this chapter emphasised the importance of the
child's family in providing care and protection in situations of
conflict and displacement. Unaccompanied children may be
especially vulnerable on two counts: first the circumstances of separation or loss of parents may have been exceptionally traumatic (e.g.
witnessing the death of parents or experiencing sudden and
unexpected separation). Second, they will be trying to survive
without the support, care and protection of familiar carers.

Some recent refugee situations have been characterised by exceptionally large numbers of children who are either orphans, or who have become separated from their families prior to or during flight. In one of the camps for Rwandese refugees in Karagwe, Tanzania[56], for example, it was found that 16 per cent of all the children had been separated from their families, about half of whom were now living with unrelated families. A survey revealed that 29 per cent of the separated children had seen their parents being killed and 63 per cent had witnessed other killings.

A full discussion of the wide range of problems associated with separated children is beyond the scope of this book and can be found in various other publications[57]. Four points emerge from the collection of case studies in this volume as being particularly significant for the psycho–social well–being of unaccompanied children.

1. Assistance for unaccompanied refugee children is an urgent priority

The case study on the work of the Standby Team strongly emphasises the urgency of programmes to provide care for separated children, and to trace parents and other family members with a view to arranging family reunification. The following extract illustrates this point:

BOX 13: THE IMPORTANCE OF EARLY WORK WITH UNACCOMPANIED CHILDREN IN EMERGENCIES[58]

"Apart from the extreme anxiety and distress faced by separated children and their families, memories of the circumstances of separation from their families will fade and the practical difficulties in tracing families will be greater. Moreover, children placed with other families will develop new attachments, and the likely disruption to those attachments caused by family reunification will increase as time passes."

2. It is important to avoid the unnecessary separation of children from their families

The case study on the work of the Standby Team also offers a dramatic example of how misguided attempts to help children can actually result in the unnecessary and damaging separation of children from their parents or others who have assumed responsibility for their care.

The work of Rädda Barnen's Swedish Department, and their research into the situation of unaccompanied African refugee children in Sweden[59] has resulted in an awareness of the particular problems facing children and young people who have sought refuge in Sweden without their families and have subsequently experienced a wide range of severe difficulties, including the problem of finding ways of being reunited with them.

There is a vital role for agencies in promoting family unity by supporting families, preventing unnecessary and inappropriate separations as well as taking urgent steps to reunite separated children as quickly as possible.

3. All aspects of work with unaccompanied children need to be carefully integrated

The case study on the work of the Standby Team illustrates the difficulties created when different agencies have different functions which are not carefully coordinated, leading to a situation in which important decisions about the child's present care and future plans were not being based around the totality of the child's experience. This places at serious risk the important principle of actions being taken in the best interests of the child[60]. In contrast, the case study on the Unaccompanied Children[61] from South Sudan illustrates well the beneficial effects of a close and careful integration of all aspects of life for this large group of unaccompanied refugee children – care arrangements, preventive mental health programmes, education and contact with their families.

4. Care arrangements for unaccompanied children need to be based on a clear understanding of the culture and traditions of the particular refugee population

Although, as a general principle, it is not in the interests of children to be placed in institutional care unless all other options have been carefully considered, placing children in foster care with unrelated caregivers may be an unfamiliar practice and consequently may involve an element of risk. In some cultures, for example, foster care may be considered appropriate but would not necessarily involve the foster child being treated in the same way as other children in the family[62].

An approach to the care of unaccompanied children which was highly sensitive to cultural traditions is illustrated in the case study on refugees from Sudan referred to above:

BOX 14: CULTURALLY APPROPRIATE CARE ARRANGEMENTS FOR UNACCOMPANIED REFUGEE CHILDREN

Many of these unaccompanied young people were accommodated in a form of group care which was adapted from the practice of boys living together in groups in cattle camps in which they exercised responsibility for themselves and for each other. However, in the Kakuma camp it was decided that some of the younger and more vulnerable children should be placed in foster homes. However, children themselves were encouraged to choose families with whom they felt an affinity, and placements were then approved and supported by refugee social workers. Some families offered minimal support and supervision (e.g. to older boys) while in other situations foster care involved full integration with the host family.

Conclusions

Unaccompanied children who have had traumatic experiences of conflict, separation and flight are clearly to be regarded as potentially the most vulnerable of all refugees. It is unlikely that such children will be able to benefit from whatever resources may facilitate psychological recovery unless and until their current needs for care, personal support and protection are met. The provision of a caring and nurturing family, or, in some situations, membership of a small and supportive peer group living environment, is clearly the first and urgent priority, and as far as possible, integrated with other forms of social support which may facilitate emotional recovery from traumatising experiences.

This chapter has also considered the support needs of families, emphasising the importance of social networks, especially those which offer culturally appropriate means of supporting women, restoring to the extent possible a sense of control over their own lives.

CHAPTER 6
The Importance of Play

THE CONCEPT OF children's play is of central importance in any discussion of the effects of war and displacement on children, and of strategies for responding to their needs, for two reasons.

First, the effects of traumatic experiences are often reflected in children's play. The case study on the work of Hi Neighbour in the Federal Republic of Yugoslavia illustrates this most clearly, as the following demonstates:

> ## BOX 15: CHILDREN'S PLAY AS A
> ## REFLECTION OF EXPERIENCES OF WAR
>
> In observing the effects of war on children's play, psychologists noticed that children displayed a preoccupation with war, and their reactions to it, but their playing lacked the vital ingredient of normal play which is the *elaboration* of experience. When they observed the play of children who had been more directly caught up in the war and had become refugees, they found that many children *were unable to play* and were often inhibited in their expression of emotion.

A similar observation comes from Elizabeth Jareg[63]: "Almost everybody is silent, even children, apart from sore, persistent crying. People's faces wear a dazed, distant or constantly distressed look. People sit motionless, staring ahead, or with their faces covered, as if trying to hide within themselves. Children sit as close up to their mother or father as possible; they do not play". Children's play is impeded not only by direct experiences of war, but also by poverty, hunger and disruption to their lives.

Restoring playfulness can be seen, then, as a sign of the beginning of children's recovery from traumatic experiences, but it is also an important means of facilitating recovery. This links with the *second* reason why play is so important: It is a vital factor in children's development, cognitively, emotionally and socially. Play is a means by which children handle and work on experiences and tackle difficult problems. Although play, like the concept of childhood itself, is firmly rooted in culture, the importance of play transcends cultural variations. Jan Williamson[64] sums up the importance of play thus: "Play for children is the major vehicle for expression of feelings and integration of difficult life experiences. Despite cultural variations, repetitive play, role modelling, fantasy and re–enactments of daily life, are all integral to the development of children worldwide. *They are essential needs of refugee children.*" (italics original).

Several of the case studies in this book illustrate different approaches to the use of play to facilitate children's recovery from difficult experiences. In the early stages of the Rwandan refugee emergency[65], considerable importance was attached to the re–establishing of activities for children and young people – whether in the form of cultural and recreational activities, sports or informal schools. The need to provide space for children's play in refugee camps should always be an important consideration in the early planning of the camp. However, in the context of so many competing priorities for the attention of Community Service Officers in the emergency phase, it was nor always possible to make as much progress in promoting recreational activities as the situation really demanded.

In the more established refugee camp situation depicted in the case study on Somali refugees in Yemen[66], the use of play and activities was the medium chosen by the refugee teachers as the most appropriate means of enabling children to express their feelings, and to communicate with others regarding the difficult experiences that they had both in Somalia and subsequently in becoming caught up in the war in Yemen. This programme is depicted in Box 7 on page 32.

In Yugoslavia, Hi Neighbour use a workshop approach with both adults and children to provide a means by which refugees can interact together and find means of examining and working on the many issues facing them in their human development. A wide variety of games, compiling and peforming stories, drawing and other "playful" media are used as a means of enabling them to express themselves, share experiences and discover and mobilise their own personal resources.

It should be emphasised that this approach is far removed from the concept of play therapy: Hi Neighbour's approach is based on developmental psychology and the notion that children will spontaneously tackle difficult issues through their play. The role of the psychologists in this programme is not to provide treatment, but to provide the "tools" with which children can express themselves and handle the reality they are facing.

Play is also an important theme in the work of the National Children and Violence Trust in South Africa[67]. Much of their work focuses on mobilising a wide range of "healing resources" which already exist within local communities, and particular importance is attached to using traditional forms of play which can be used as a means of enabling children to express themselves in a culturally appropriate way.

A final example of the use of play in assisting children affected by war and displacement is the dance, drama and classical music workshops promoted by Rädda Barnen's Swedish Programme[68]. Here again, a variety of "playful" media are used to facilitate self–expression (especially important for children with a limited knowledge of Swedish) and to enable children to work on the many problems and issues they face in their changing lives.

Play often serves as a useful "barometer" of children's well–being. The contents of play may indicate the issues and problems which preoccupy them, while the style and manner of playing can give an indication of the extent to which children have been impaired by their experiences.

Children who are unable to play may be particularly at risk: not only does this inability indicate that the child is profoundly affected by his/her experiences, but the inability to play means that the child no longer has access to the natural healing properties of play. For these reasons, the early provision of opportunities for children to play, to meet together and socialise with each other, and to engage in purposeful activity is of vital importance in refugee emergencies: "If children are given the possibilities for play together with other children and adults, children can then use their own power and thereby get possibilities to grow even during very difficult circumstances"[69]. The restoration of cultural and community activities are important, as well as the early moves to implement pre–school and school programmes. The contribution of schools to the psychological well–being of children is the subject of the next chapter.

CHAPTER 7

The Role of Schools
and Teachers

THE RESEARCH LITERATURE on resilience in children places central
importance on the existence of appropriate networks which provide
social supports for children. Clearly the child's own, or substitute,
family is usually the single most significant source of support, but
after the family, it is the school which probably has the greatest
capacity for providing children with a range of experiences which
serve in a supportive capacity.

In most communities, the school is the public service structure
which reaches the largest number of children, and it is teachers who
have the most close and frequent contact with them apart from
family members. Moreover, in some cultures, teachers get to know
families closely, as well as children, and they may carry a great deal of
authority and respect within the wider community. It is therefore
not surprising to find that schools are often seen as a vital source of
personal and emotional support to children affected by their
experiences of war and displacement, apart from their primary task
of providing education in its more traditional sense.

On the other hand, in some cultures, education does not receive
a high priority, especially for girls. Moreover, in some conflict
situations (for example Mozambique and Liberia), schools were
particular targets for military activity.

The Eriksonian child development framework outlined earlier
emphasised the key themes of trust, competence, identity and
meaning. Schools and pre–schools provide vital settings for the
promoting of child development. Regular attendance and

meaningful contact with teachers and other children help to re-create a sense of *trust and stability*. Scholastic achievement enhances children's sense of *competence* and this, coupled with the formal and informal social interaction which schools offer assists in the forma-tion of a strong sense of *personal identity*. Providing schooling demonstrates society's recognition of the value of children, collectively and individually, which contributes to self–esteem. It gives them a hope for the future and a confidence in their own survival. Finally, schools can provide a situation in which young people can talk about shared experiences and integrate the *meaning* of events into their view of themselves and their world.

This chapter seeks to analyse the role played by schools in meeting the psycho–social needs of children, drawing on the experience of the seven case studies. This experience suggests that the part played by schools can be grouped under seven main headings:

1. Identifying vulnerable children, assessing their needs and monitoring their progress

Teachers may be the only professional group to have regular contact with children who are affected by their experiences of war and dis-placement, and their knowledge of child development places them in a central role for identifying vulnerable children. Teachers can readily be trained in the signs and symptoms of stress in children, and are well placed to monitor the development and progress of children whose well–being has been affected by their experiences.

However, teachers will not necessarily be well placed to respond to the emotional needs of children (see point 4 below), and assessing their needs and monitoring their progress will only be useful if either they are able to provide appropriate responses themselves, or have other resources available to which to refer.

2. Providing a daily structure, purpose and meaning for children

One of the most obvious impacts of both conflict and displacement is that they tend to disrupt or even destroy social institutions such as schools. Refugee children in particular have experienced wholesale disruption in their lives – the loss of familiar people and surroundings (including parents and family members), loss of a sense of order and structure and predictability to their lives, loss of a clear sense of their future.

Reviewing the research stemming from experiences of war zones in Europe during the Second World War, Neil Boothby[70] writes: "Children exposed to air raids not only benefitted from the presence of parents, but from the presence of teachers, neighbours, extended family and other familiar adults. These adults provide children with a representation of their own abilities to exert inner control in the midst of chaotic and changing circumstances". This conclusion is equally relevant to contemporary refugee emergencies.

The early weeks and months in a refugee camp may be characterised by an overwhelming sense of loss and shock, which can be followed by an equally damaging sense of despair and resignation, unless steps are taking quickly to restore a structure and purpose in their lives. This is where an early start to provide education can be so important. Education is almost always identified by refugees themselves as an urgent priority, and this was particularly illustrated in the case study on the work of the Standby Team[71], from which the following quotation is taken:

> **BOX 16: THE PRIORITY OF EDUCATION IN REFUGEE ENERGENCIES**
>
> "The real significance of early initiatives to begin educational activities lies in the urgency to create for children, especially those who have been distressed by their experiences, *a structure to their daily lives, a sense of purpose, and the rewards of achievement* and the self–esteem that result from it. Participation in educational activities

also provides young people not only with a sense of future, but an opportunity themselves to invest in that future. This is vital in helping to avoid that passive dependence and sense of hopelessness and despair that can so easily characterise refugee camps. It is with these objectives in mind that educational activity is so valuable, long before the stage where it is possible to implement more formal education....".

The case study on the Unaccompanied Children of South Sudan[72] used similar terminology in emphasising the importance of structure and routine in the lives of this large group of unaccompanied children.

Another aspect of the maintenance of a sense of order in children's lives, especially for refugee children, is the preservation of culture and traditions, of values and practice, all of which provide a continuous link with the past and an investment in the future.

3. Enhancing children's understanding of events

Western therapeutic approaches emphasise the value of "talking through" experiences in order to enable individuals to understand and make sense of them. The value of this cognitive and integrative function of therapy probably does have trans–cultural importance. But an individual professional relationship with a therapist or counsellor is but one of many ways by which this need can be met. In situations in which children have shared stressful experiences with their families, their peers or indeed the whole community, it is more likely that talking about and developing understanding of such experiences will most effectively occur with others who have shared them.

Schools can play a vital role in enabling children to discuss experiences of violence, danger, displacement etc., and in so doing develop both individual and shared understanding of the meaning of these events. It is in this context that the teaching of such subjects as history and geography can have particular relevance, especially for refugee children. In the Kakuma camp[73], for example, it was decided to base the curriculum on the Kenyan model, but to include as a specific topic the history of South Sudan. It is, however, important that the teaching of such subjects is undertaken in a way that promotes dialogue and discussion, not merely conveying factual information, in order to enable children to "process" information and make sense of it in their own lives.

Religious and political beliefs also contribute to the process of understanding and making sense of difficult experiences. Although this is sometimes a controversial area for schools, there are many ways in which they contribute to young people's understanding of events and experiences. Religious education and the teaching of "civics" (or its equivalent) may be particularly important, but also on an informal level, schools provide opportunity for peer–group discussions which may be just as significant.

However, in refugee situations, there are often sensitivities and conflicts, especially regarding curricula, with the host government, the refugees themselves and possibly the government of the country of origin expressing different ideas, values and priorities. Reaching agreement on areas such as curricula and the recruiting and payment of teachers can be difficult.

4. Providing avenues for the expression of feelings and opportunities for more personal support

A number of programmes worldwide have particularly sought to develop the role of the teacher in order to provide more personalised support to children, both in refugee situations and in countries affected by civil war. At the most simple level, teachers can act as good role models for children, offering a concern for their wellbeing and a context in which they can feel accepted and valued. Some programmes have attempted to go further than this in giving teachers a more specific role in dealing with psycho–social needs; however, it is clear that these programmes have not been uniformly successful.

This collection of case studies illustrates a number of different approaches to the involvement of schools in this wider role with children. One of the most interesting describes the role of education in a camp for Somali refugees in Yemen[74]:

BOX 17: THE CENTRAL ROLE OF A SCHOOL IN PROVIDING PSYCHOSOCIAL CARE

Rädda Barnen was involved in initiating a school which had, as an expressed purpose, to meet some of the psycho–social needs of children affected by their experiences of war and displacement. The original intention was to equip teachers with the knowledge and skills required to enable them to lead group discussions and to carry out "supportive conversations" with individual children.

For various reasons this training was not provided. Instead the teachers developed their own distinctive methodology, based on the cultural norm of not discussing painful issues directly. They developed a range of extra–curricular activities for children, some of which also involved parents. These included singing, drama, story–telling, sports and games, and through these media teachers encouraged the expression of feelings and verbal communication in a culturally–appropriate manner and in the context of a supportive and accepting community ethos.

In this situation, it is clear that the teachers had highly significant roles and status within the refugee community and had succeeded in developing the school into the most important social structure in the camp, extending the role of teachers beyond the school and out into the community.

Other attempts to develop the role of the teacher to meet the psycho–social needs of war–affected children have been less successful. In Malawi[75], for example, an attempt was made to train teachers in the many camps for Mozambican refugees in what was described as "psycho–social rehabilitation". Again the intention was to provide them with the skills to undertake individual counselling and group activities. Two particular factors were identified as leading to the disappointing impact of the programme: first, the very limited teacher training programme provided. Second the lack of opportunities to enable the teachers to examine their own experiences and feelings in order to free them to work constructively at an emotional level with children. The importance of providing support to staff undertaking this kind of work will be discussed further in chapter 10.

Two additional factors also seem to be important when this experience is compared with that described in Box 17 above. First, in a culture in which teaching methods are very formal and non–interactive, and teacher–centred rather than child–centred, Mozambican teachers were being asked to work in a way which was in striking contrast with the culture of their profession and which probably posed a challenge to their professional self–concept. By way of contrast, in the Yemeni camps, conscious steps were taken to recruit, as teachers, members of the refugee community chosen for their personal qualities which would enable them to work in a very different way with children than was typical of teachers. Interestingly, in the classroom situation they continued to operate in a traditional, "top–down" and non–interactive mode, but outside of the classroom they proved able to work in an informal, interactive and highly supportive manner.

Second, there was a tendency in the Mozambican situation to assume the cultural relevance and appropriateness of promoting an approach which relied on the more direct expression of feelings and talking about experiences (see discussion of this issue in chapter 2). One of the dangers of western models of intervention is that they can easily be uncritically accepted on a superficial level but not really become integrated into the working practices of the professionals concerned. A particular strength of the approach taken in Yemen was that it was developed by the teachers themselves. This served to greatly enhance their commitment to it and their sense of ownership of it.

A quite different approach to using the school as a forum for psycho–social intervention is illustrated in the case study of the Rädda Barnen Swedish Department[76]. One component of the programme is the development of dance and drama workshops in schools and pre–schools. They are conducted by specially trained pedagogues, and provide opportunities for children from refugee backgrounds to express themselves in a variety of non–verbal ways, to learn new methods of communication, to work on their difficult past experiences and to examine their current difficulties – all in a relaxing and enjoyable atmosphere. These experiences seemed to have the greatest impact in situations where the school teachers worked closely with the pedagogues in order to integrate the themes and issues emerging from the workshops into their classroom work with children.

This issue of *integration* is central in developing the role of teachers with the broader psycho–social needs of children. The case study on the Unaccompanied Children from South Sudan[77] provides an illustration of the way in which care arrangements, community activities and educational experiences formed an integrated preventive mental health programme. This was in striking contrast to many of the refugee camps in Malawi[78]: while teachers became effective in recognising the signs of stress in children, they lacked the skills and methods to deal with these themselves. Moreover, there was a lack of other resources to which they could refer.

5. The role of schools in contributing to the broader education of children and others in the community

Schools also have a potential role in providing education more broadly within the community. Child–to–child approaches have become increasingly popular, particularly in promoting health education in refugee camps. "Child–to–Child and Children in Camps"[79], for example, includes a chapter on "Helping Children who Experience War, Disaster or Conflict". Some schools have pioneered the production of a newsletter – for example the school featured in Box 17 above.

In South Africa, the case study on the NCVT[80] provides an example of the role of the school in becoming a vehicle for public education. Schools, youth clubs and women's organisations are particularly targeted as forums for training and the promotion of awareness about such issues as the different manifestations of violence, the effects of violence and trauma on people and the need for non–violent means of conflict resolution.

In El Salvador, the village–level volunteer Promoters deployed by Acisam[81] were involved in education in schools, dealing with such topics as grief and loss, alcoholism, domestic violence and other subjects falling broadly under the heading of preventive mental health. It was Acisam's experience that children were frequently seen to be more open to change and new ideas than were adults. By working directly with young people it was hoped that their work would indirectly impact on their parents and other adults within the community.

6. The development of schools as a vehicle for community mobilisation and development

Schools are more than places for educating children. In new refugee camps, education is often seen by the refugees as first priority and frequently the initial planning of education serves as a vehicle by which people come together to plan. Schools are symbolic of both collectivity and stability; they demonstrate a community investment in the future and symbolise a sense of hope.

In conflict zones, too, education has a value well beyond the immediate benefits to children. Margaret Akello Kenyi[82], in a paper presented to a recent conference said: "In Southern Sudan, one of the signs of hope for future generations is a gathering of children and some adults, most often under trees, around an ill–equipped volunteer teacher". In post–conflict situations, the building of school premises may symbolise a return to normality, a sign of permanence and hope.

Members of Rädda Barnen's Standby Team often found

education to be the issue around which refugees could most readily be engaged in collective responsibility and activity, with the formation of an Education Committee comprising the first and important step towards re–establishing education in refugee camps. Once established, a school may continue to contribute to community development by being a highly significant focal point for children, for parents and very often for the whole community. The school described in the case study on the Yemen (see Box 17) graphically illustrates how the camp school became a vibrant resource, the most significant social structure in the camp which met human needs far above and beyond those met by the traditional school.

7. The role of the school in promoting reconciliation

Civil war inevitably creates distrust and divisions within local communities, for example between people with differing political allegiances, or between those who fled and those who remained. Direct involvement in violence – as illustrated most graphically in Rwanda and Bosnia – creates particularly powerful tensions.

Schools can have a vital role in facilitating reconciliation between children, with the potential of having a wider impact within the community. Naomi Richman et al[83] talk of the role of teachers with children and parents in helping to reintegrate children who had been recruited into the guerilla army in Mozambique. Acisam in El Salvador found that children were frequently less polarised in their views than were adults: their director referred to children and youth as being "the new actors in the new reality", and it was frequently found that it was through young people that work towards reconciliatation between adults could be undertaken. Similarly, in the refugee camp for Somalis in Yemen, the camp school seemed able to work effectively to promote reconciliation between people from different tribal groups, providing a "free zone" despite the existence of tribal conflicts within the community.

Conclusions

Rädda Barnen's experience clearly demonstrates that schools do and must play a central role in assisting children whose psycho–social well–being has been adversely affected by war or displacement. Indeed it would be difficult to see how any strategy could ignore the central role that schools and pre–schools play in the lives of children. At the same time, the experience outlined in this chapter offers some notes of caution.

First, it must be remembered that not all children attend school. The signs of traumatic stress in children include those of depression, withdrawal and social isolation (see Box 3 on page 8). Consequently, some of the most needy children may not be attending school, but quietly suffering in isolation from the world outside the home. For this reason, programmes which rely exclusively on school–based interventions may completely miss a significant, and potentially high–risk part of their target–group. Moreover, in many situations, schools have a marked *gender imbalance*, sometimes with only a small minority of girls attending.

Conversely, in some situations of conflict it has been found that boarding schools often have an unusually high concentration of children who have been psychologically affected by war. In Serbia, for example, boarding schools often contained a high percentage of refugee children, the boarding school effectively becoming "home" for children unable to return to their families during the holidays.

Second, insofar as school–based programmes rely on a major shift in the traditional role, knowledge and skills of teachers, it is vital to avoid the naive assumption that teachers can take on tasks which, in some respects, conflict with the role–relationship between teachers and pupils which may be characteristic of some traditional approaches to education. What has sometimes, perhaps, been seen as "adding on" additional tasks may, in reality, involve a major change in the role and self–concept of the teacher.

Third, experience in Mozambique and Malawi highlights the fact that teachers as well as children have psycho–social needs arising from their own experiences of conflict and displacement. It is unlikely that teachers will be in a position to assist children constructively unless they have been able to face and deal with their own personal problems. There is an obvious danger that otherwise they may use discussions with children as a means of gaining support for themselves rather than providing it for them. It is vital that adequate training, personal preparation and on–going support are provided if teachers are going to be able to provide adequate help and support to vulnerable children. This issue will be discussed further in chapter 10.

Finally, an educational resource oriented to the broader psycho–social needs of children is most likely to be effective if it is closely integrated with other community resources. The case studies based on experience in Yemen[84] and Ethiopia/Kenya[85] both illustrate the considerable impact that schools can have on children's sense of well–being when their work is embedded in the life of the community as a whole.

CHAPTER 8

The Need for Timely
Intervention

WORK IN A refugee emergency raises a dilemma: should early interventions focus primarily on what is *important* or only on what is *urgent*? Jan Williamson, in referring to the general lack of psycho–social programmes, talks about "myths that have grown up around children within refugee emergencies. The belief is common among relief organisations that efforts to address the psycho–social needs of refugee children are "luxuries" that might be nice but are not really needed"[86]. Unfortunately, the view expressed in this quotation is still widespread, though thankfully this is now changing.

Frequently it is the most urgent concerns that generally demand priority, and while it is difficult to argue against prioritising work which saves and preserves life, it is increasingly being recognised that psycho–social needs are both important and urgent.

It has long been realised that there is a "critical period" following a crisis during which psychological intervention is particularly important[87]. It is during this quite short period that people tend to develop a variety of different psychologial responses, some of which may be healthy and appropriate, others may be disfunctional (e.g. apathy and helplessness); there is a real danger that the latter become entrenched and difficult to change. Referring to immigrants to Israel after 1948, Caplan observed the long–term effects of apathy and dependence: "Many of them had sunk into an apathetic, dependent state, and when the opportunity for independent and self–respecting work arrived many could not grasp it"[88].

The Standby Team is attempting to address issues which, though not immediately saving lives, are of vital importance to the long–term well–being of refugees. In the process, they are helping to draw attention to the fact that psycho–social needs are also urgent. The urgency, for example, in responding to the needs of unaccompanied refugee children was discussed in Chapter 5, but more broadly it has been realised that there are long–term benefits in mobilising refugees early on to take responsibility for identifying needs and planning programmes, and for a range of self–help activities. The case study on the work of the Standby Team[89] takes the view that, far from being a "luxury", the early deployment of a Community Services Officer is both effective and cost–effective, as the following quotation indicates:

BOX 18: THE IMPORTANCE OF EARLY PSYCHO–SOCIAL INTERVENTION IN REFUGEE EMERGENCIES

"The deployment of a CSO in an emergency can be seen as a very cost–effective measure.....The community mobilisation approach, in contrast with the traditional individually oriented social work approach, means that large numbers of refugees can be reached without the necessity of deploying large numbers of specialist staff to undertake direct work with children and families. The approach has the great advantage of *capacitating both refugees themselves, and local NGOs* in such a way that their own resources are strengthened by new knowledge, skills and experience. The active engagement with refugees is highly significant in helping to avoid the passive dependence which can have extremely serious and long–term consequences; and while refugee empowerment and mobilisation are, by their nature, difficult to measure, the effects were to be seen in Karagwe".

The case study on the work of Hi Neighbour in the Federal Republic of Yugoslavia also draws attention to the advantages of working with people as soon as possible after becoming refugees. Their psychologists found that in this early phase, though many refugees were distressed and anxious, they observed "the release of a great deal of *creative energy* among the refugees, despite the exceptionally difficult circumstances they had experienced and the current stresses and privations they were faced with"[90]. The longer–term benefits of the refugees exercising a high level of self–responsibility from the early stage of a refugee emergency are demonstrated by the case study on refugees from South Sudan[91].

Return from refuge can also be seen as a "critical period" in the lives of people affected by conflict and displacement. The work of Acisam[92] in El Salvador demonstrated clearly that people's psychological responses to the *conflict* were inextricably mixed with their responses to the *peace*. It was during the difficult period following the peace agreement that many people had to grapple not only with their personal and collective experiences of the conflict, but also with the widespread sense of disappointment with the terms of the settlement, and the continuing problems of inequality, poverty, injustice and abuses of human rights. It is an unfortunate fact that there is frequently an exodus of aid agencies following the end of conflicts: Rädda Barnen's experience suggests that the opportunities for timely and appropriate intervention may exist during this critical period as well as in the early stages in a refugee emergency.

Critical life experiences can prompt a whole range of inappropriate responses – emotional withdrawal, social isolation, dependency, restrictive child care practices (such as over–protection), and so on. Such reactions may, in the short term, help to protect people from the immediate impact of traumatic events, but in the long–term are likely to impede healthy adjustment and development. But, as James Garbarino et al. point out[93], "situations of chronic danger can stimulate the process of moral development if they are matched by an interactive climate created by adults (and endorsed – or at least not stifled – by the larger culture through its political, educational, and religious institutions) and if the child is free of debilitating psychopathology". An important task of agencies involved in critical phases of emergencies is to help to create this "interactive climate" in which people are encouraged to work actively on the problems and issues confronting them. This, perhaps, is the most valuable contribution of members of the Standby Team: if successful, it is difficult to envisage a more cost–effective and sustainable use of resources – themes which will be pursued further in the next chapter.

CHAPTER 9

Strategies for Achieving Maximum Coverage, Impact and Sustainability

PSYCHO–SOCIAL PROGRAMMES can be based on very different objectives: some, for example, may see their purpose as alleviating the immediate suffering of people psychologicaly affected by their experiences of war or displacement. Others will set their sights on long–term development, with an emphasis on assisting people within the broader social, economic, cultural and political context. The former approach is often associated with the targetting of relatively small numbers of people who have been most seriously affected by their experiences (the Centre for Children Affected by Armed Conflict in Sweden[94] is an example of this kind of programme). Generally the more Western models tend to focus on the most seriously affected individuals.

The community–development approach is illustrated by the work of Acisam[95] in El Salvador, which attempts to diffuse psychological understanding more broadly within local communities and use a variety of strategies for improving the mental health of those psychologically affected by their experiences both of war and of the wide range of other obstacles to their personal and community development.

Neither of these contrasting approaches is necessarily better than the other. It depends on the overall and long–term objectives and the wider context of the work. Neither are they necessarily to be

73

seen as alternatives. The National Children and Violence Trust, for example, tries to respond to the "challenge not only to heal the wounds but to work towards an establishment of a new society where each child will be guaranteed happiness, security and freedom"[96]. Similarly, the work of the Swedish Department of Rädda Barnen is characterised by a multi–faceted approach, with its more clinical work complemented by a wide range of other strategies.

Increasingly, development programmes are being judged on the criterion on *sustainability* – i.e. the extent to which the programmes can be sustained to provide long–term benefit without a continuing high level of external funding.

Another issue confronting agencies concerned with impacting on the psycho–social well–being of people affected by war or displacement is that of *coverage*. In the case of large–scale emergencies (such as the genocide in Rwanda, the consequent exodus of people into neighbouring countries and the large numbers of people who have experienced brutal killings and multiple bereavements and separations), the problem of defining appropriate and *affordable* responses so as to reach the maximum possible number of people is a challenging one.

Where sustainability, coverage and affordability are important criteria, various approaches may be considered, some of which are illustrated by case studies in this book. They include the following strategies:

1. The Use of Volunteers

The first strategy is the deployment of *volunteers* within the community to undertake the main functions of the agency: Acisam in El Salvador provides an excellent example:

BOX 19: THE DEPLOYMENT OF
VOLUNTEER PROMOTERS IN THE
COMMUNITY

Most of the work of Acisam is carried out by a large
number of volunteer Promoters deployed within village
communities, who are trained and supported by a cadre of
full–time Facilitators, most of whom are psychologists.
Most of the Promoters work on a part–time basis,
combining their mental health promotional work with
other tasks (e.g. community midwife, popular educator
etc.). They are recruited within their own communities
and usually are already exercising some form of community
leadership. They are entirely unpaid, which enables
Acisam to work in a large number of communities in a
cost–effective manner.

A possible future development is to use some of the
more experienced Promoters as "Multipliers" who would
take on the role of training and supporting other Promoters, enabling the organisation to reach additional
communities.

The Hi Neighbour programme in Yugoslavia also achieves greater
affordability by deploying psychologists on a semi–volunteer basis.
Their work tends to operate over long time–scales, with the clear
intention of continuing their workshop groups for as long as refugees
continue to be present in the Collective Centres. Their reliance on
qualified psychologists to conduct these workshops makes the model
difficult to replicate in most developing world contexts, but by
deploying psychologists on a part–time, minimally–paid basis they
are able to achieve greater coverage and at less cost than if they had
to employ their staff on a full–time, paid basis.

Deploying volunteers is not, of course, without its difficulties.
Providing some form of incentive for volunteers is often a difficult
and controversial area, but without some form of remuneration some
projects have difficulty in recruiting volunteers. Acisam is faced
with this problem and is considering involving Promoters in

income–generating activities in order to benefit them personally as well as others in their communities.

2. Networking

A second strategy is based on networking, an approach which involves bringing together various individuals and agencies to work together to make optimum use of existing resources. This is an approach which has been particularly developed by the National Children and Violence Trust in South Africa[97]:

BOX 20: A NETWORKING APPROACH

The main thrust of the work of this organisation is the establishment and support of *community–based networks*, whose task is to identify and examine the problems of violence within the local community and to take whatever steps are required to respond to them. These may include, for example, counselling children and families, violence prevention in local schools, public awareness campaigns and so on.

Training is provided in the form of participative workshops which enable those involved in the networks to understand the problems of violence in society, to examine their own personal reactions to violence and to identify appropriate means of responding to it in the context of the particular local situation.

This networking approach provides a means of creating public awareness and diffusing psychological understandings throughout the local community in a cost–effective way.

3. Preventive Strategies

A third means of achieving greater coverage and sustainability consists of adopting preventive approaches. An example of this is provided by the Swedish programme of Rädda Barnen:

Rädda Barnen have identified that one of the principal
problems facing refugees and immigrants is societal attitudes of racism and xenophobia. In order to combat these
phenomena, it was decided to instigate a training
programme with the aim of educating pre–school teachers
and aides for working in an international, multi–cultural
society, and to instill in young children attitudes of
tolerance and the value of cultural differences. This
approach will potentially reach very large numbers of
children within Swedish society.

One area of difficulty with such an approach is that the impact of
this work will only be seen in the long term, and it is, of course,
difficult to measure the impact and to establish a causal link between
this work and the intended impact on societal attitudes. On the
other hand, it seeks to get to the roots of this particular problem
which in the long term is far more constructive than simply helping
refugees to find ways of responding appropriately when faced with
racist attitudes.

4. Advocacy

A final strategy for maximising coverage and achieving sustainable
change is that of *advocacy*. Many of the programmes included in this
collection of case studies include advocacy as part of their work, and
this is again illustrated by reference to the work of Rädda Barnen's
Swedish Department.

As a children's rights agency, Rädda Barnen has been
involved in advocacy for many years. This is pursued in a
variety of ways, ranging from sponsoring conferences and
seminars on important issues concerning people from a
refugee background, to public education: from research

and publishing work to lobbying parliament. Another aspect of their advocacy work is the programme of continuing education for professional child care workers as well as the training of pre–school staff in anti–racist practices.

The Need for Impact Evaluation

The deployment of volunteers, networking and the use of preventive and advocacy approaches have all been used as strategies for widening the impact of the work in different programmes. But one of the challenges facing all of the programmes illustrated in the seven case studies is the attempt to *measure the impact of the work*. Although most of the programmes made some attempt to evaluate their work, usually this involved the review and evaluation of the *process* rather than the *outcome*. Although it must be acknowledged that outcomes of psycho–social programmes are, almost by defini-tion, extremely difficult to measure, there is scope for working on defining qualitative and quantitative indicators which will provide a more objective picture of their impact and facilitate the process of modifying and developing the approaches used. In the context of the dearth of empirical evidence on the efficacy of different approaches to assisting people whose lives have been affected by war and displacement, this would make an important contribution to the building of knowledge in this difficult area.

Each of the programmes illustrated in this collection of case studies is a product of its particular social, economic and cultural context. Clearly what is an appropriate approach in one context may be quite unsuited to another. For example, the more clinical ap-proach adopted in the Centre for Children Affected by Armed Conflict in Sweden would not be appropriate in Rwanda, not only because of the cultural issues discussed in Chapter 1, but because it would be patently unaffordable. In such large–scale situations, the more community–based approaches are probably the only viable ways of reaching such large numbers of people whose lives have been shattered by violence. But this book has also strongly argued that in the majority of Third World countries, more community–oriented approaches are also more appropriate. This important theme will be returned to in Chapter 11.

CHAPTER 10

Supporting Staff Involved in Psycho–social Programmes

IN COMPILING THE collection of case studies for this book, it has been striking that all of the programmes described, without exception, rely on highly committed and highly motivated front–line staff, many of whom work under difficult, and certainly sometimes dangerous conditions. Many work long hours for relatively modest payment; others receive no remuneration at all.

A particular feature of some of the programmes is the recruitment of staff or volunteers from the communities which have been directly affected by conflict or displacement. This is perhaps most graphically illustrated by the work of Acisam[98]: volunteer Promoters are recruited at village level to take on a wide range of different tasks designed to promote good mental health within their own communities. People are usually chosen because they have existing leadership roles within the community, including, for example, ex–combatants. The advantage of such an approach is that it capitalises on existing (and inside) knowledge of the local community, its needs, problems and resources. But a potential disadvantage is that those same people may be carrying the emotional burden stemming from their own experiences of the war and of the difficult conditions associated with the post–war period.

In Mozambique, and in refugee camps in Malawi, the strategy of using teachers in a caring and supportive capacity to assist children affected by their experience of the war was hampered by the fact that many of these teachers were profoundly affected by their own experiences[99]. In this particular conflict, teachers and schools had been particularly targetted for attacks by Renamo guerillas.

The work of the National Children and Violence Trust in South Africa[100] involved a considerable element of danger when township violence was widespread. The killing in 1992 of Moses Sihlangu, the first ever African clinical psychologist to work in his particular area, had a profound impact on the whole organisation.

These examples serve to illustrate the stresses – sometimes extreme stresses – which may face people involved in psycho–social programmes. Working with traumatised people, in difficult and possibly dangerous contexts, and when workers themselves have had to face their own stressful situations – all these mean that the issue of "caring for the caregivers" needs to be a central issue for any organisation involved in this area of work.

The case studies in this book illustrate a variety of approaches to this theme. The school teachers in the camp school in Yemen, for example, benefitted not only from a highly supportive working environment but from a conscious attempt by the teachers to evolve their own coping strategies as is illustrated by the following quotation from the case study[101]:

BOX 23: COPING STRATEGIES FOR CHILD CARE PROFESSIONALS

"The teachers themselves adopted a number of strategies for dealing with their own difficult experiences. These included reciting the Koran and developing their faith, learning more through reading and listening to the radio and taking part in a range of different activities".

Acisam evolved a pattern of support to their volunteer Promoters which was provided by Facilitators, most of whom are psychologists. This comprised regular supervision meetings which provided opportunities not only for planning and reviewing their work, but also for offering support. Moreover, the participatory style of training provided opportunities for Promoters to examine and share their own personal experiences.

The dangers of staff burnout and exhaustion are ever–present realities for people undertaking difficult and stressful work, with stressed people, and in difficult situations. It is important for any organisation working in this area to ensure that adequate support systems are provided. In deploying staff or volunteers, a balance needs to be found between, on the one hand the need to capitalise on the personal commitment of workers, and, on the other, the need for sensible boundaries to ensure that excessive working hours are avoided and that they have access to support which enables them to face and deal healthily with the emotional impact of their work. Failure to do so can result not only in unacceptable levels of personal stress, but also in the loss of the most valuable asset of the organisation, its skilled and committed workforce.

CHAPTER 11

Towards a Model of Community Resilience

THROUGHOUT THIS BOOK, considerable emphasis has been placed on the value of a *community perspective*. It has been suggested that in many societies, the impact of conflict and displacement is experienced in shared rather than individual terms. It is important for problems, needs and priorities to be defined by people collectively, and for responses to them to reflect the resourcefulness of the people themselves. Approaches which rely on external definitions of the problems, and a professionalisation of the means of dealing with them, carry the danger of bypassing people's own insights into the nature of the problems and their context. They may also override people's individual and collective strengths and resources; in the process, this can be disempowering and potentially damaging.

On the other hand, it is important not to make naive and universalist assumptions about the nature of "community". For example, two of the case studies in this book provide illustrations of work undertaken in social contexts where the sense of community is not very strong – Sweden and the Federal Republic of Yugoslavia. Although the work of Hi Neighbour did succeed in working with the "community" in the sense of the population of Collective Centres, it was very difficult in Yugoslavia to work with the much larger numbers of refugees living with host families using a community organisation model. Nevertheless, working with International Rescue Committee, Hi Neighbour is now adopting an approach designed to reach refugees living with host families using a community–centre approach offering a range of resources to both refugees and their host families. Early results from this approach are encouraging.

A second possible limitation of a community–based approach is that in some societies, especially in Asia, the sense of community is profoundly affected by the social divisions of religion, social class and caste, making it difficult to work collectively and cooperatively with the people living in a specified location: "community" perhaps needs to be defined more in terms of a group of people sharing particular needs, problems or resources who can be brought together to pursue shared goals.

A third limitation to the community–based approach is to be seen in some refugee camps, and possibly other politicised communities affected by conflict. Community action to promote healing or resilience may be impeded by political divisions, or by highly polarised political views such as those in evidence in some of the Rwandese refugee camps, especially in Zaire.

A final potential limitation of approaches which emphasise collective responses is that they raise the difficult question of how to reach those people who have been so profoundly affected by their experiences that they are unable to take part in collective activity. Rädda Barnen's experience suggest that the numbers so affected are likely to be much smaller than some would expect. Their work in Pignudo and Kakuma, for example, suggests that the community–based approach taken was effective in assisting all but a tiny minority of these young people, despite the exceptional experiences of violence, danger, hardship, separation and repeated displacement.

Some would argue that however effective the approaches based on collective action, there will always be a need for more specialised psychological and psychiatric facilities to reach those who cannot benefit from community–based methods. However, in the developing world it is extremely difficult to find modern psychiatric clinics and hospitals in which it is possible to feel confident about the outcome of the treatment approaches being offered. This is not an argument against developing good psychiatric facilities, but rather an acknowledgement that such developments require, first, a thorough understanding of cultural issues, and second sufficient human and material resources to be effective. In the contexts of most developing countries, it is difficult to argue in favour of clinical facilities when their high cost and questionable cultural relevance are taken into account, especially in situations where more community–oriented approaches are possible.

So although care must be taken to avoid the assumptions that community–based programmes offer a panacea to all psycho–social problems the world over, it must also be recognised that the majority of conflicts in recent times have occurred in societies in which community–based approaches appear to offer the most appropriate, sustainable and affordable way forward. Some of the characteristic features of these approaches were indicated in Box 6 on page 25, and some of their advantages are summarised below:

1. They are based on *definitions of needs, problems and priorities made by the people themselves*. This is in striking contrast to the "top down" approach which is sometimes advocated by those espousing a more clinical approach[102]. The importance of community definitions of problems and needs are particularly emphasised in the case studies in Acisam in El Salvador and the National Children and Violence Trust in South Africa.

2. They are based on *traditional methods* of coping with adversity and on *existing strengths and resources* within individuals and within the community, rather than seeking to replace (and potentially undermine) them. The case study on the Unaccompanied Refugee Children from Sudan illustrates this theme particularly well.

3. They adopt *participative methods, and thereby empower people*, giving them more control over their own lives. The importance of participation and empowerment has been stressed throughout this book and is illustrated by many of the case studies.

4. By adopting a *holistic approach*, they enable a focus on issues stemming from past experiences, on current areas of stress and difficulty and on future developments within the community.

Again, the importance of the wider social, economic, cultural and political context has been stressed in many of the case studies.

5. This approach contributes to the *long–term development* of the community rather than merely attempting to relieve immediate

distress. This may be especially important for agencies who are committed to long–term, sustainable development within local communities.

6. Community–based programmes which adopt networking approaches tend to be *highly cost effective*, potentially reaching large numbers of people at relatively modest cost. Issues of sustainability and cost–effectiveness were discussed in more detail in Chapter 9.

7. By embracing either whole communities, or significant sections of communities, they *avoid the stigmatising effect* of isolating people on the grounds of "being traumatised", "pathological" etc.. No rigid distinction needs to be made between prevention and treatment. Rather the assumption is that whole communities are affected by experiences of war and displacement, and that all can benefit from programmes which address these issues in the wider context of the life situation of the community as a whole. Another advantage is that people who may currently display no symptoms of stress may be able to benefit from the approach.

8. Similarly, they seek to *promote psychological understandings broadly throughout the community*, ideally avoiding the specialised language of psychology and psychiatry. This helps to generate an ethos which sees psycho–social well–being as everybody's responsibility, not just that of specialists and of external agents.

The concept of *resilience* was introduced in Chapter 2, and has been used to describe the characteristics of individuals who seem most able to cope healthily with high levels of stress, though emphasis was placed on protective factors within the wider social milieu which contribute to the resilience of individuals.

It may, however, be helpful to apply the concept of resilience to whole communities. The case study on the work of Acisam[103] in El Salvador includes a brief description of a particular village community which could be described as resilient, and similarly the work of the Standby Team functions in a way which encourages community resilience. So what are the typical characteristics of a resilient community? Although no definitive answers can be provided, Rädda Barnen's experiences as reviewed in the present volume suggest that the following may be particularly significant:

- there is a *strong sense of community* characterised by open relationships between people, good communication and a strong sense of collectivism.
- *leadership is democratic*, or at least leaders genuinely represent the people, and that women as well as men are able to exercise leadership functions.
- *supportive structures exist* within the locality – for example, schools and pre–schools, health services, women's groups, people's organisations, economic cooperatives and religious organisations all provide a high level of social support.
- there is a *commitment to community development*, a strong sense of the people themselves being organised to take responsibility and take action to develop and transform the lives of the inhabitants.
- problems such as the effects of conflict and displacement are widely acknowledged as *shared rather than individual problems*; psychological understandings are diffused broadly in the community and there is a commitment to developing collective responses.
- *people see themselves as resourceful*, and their communities as having the potential for meeting the needs of their people in a culturally appropriate manner, relying on external resources only when necessary.

In the context of most developing countries, it is likely that the psycho–social needs of children who are psychologically affected by war and displacement are most likely to be met by strategies which emphasise family support in the context of a community which actively seeks to address the whole range of the needs of its members – social, psychological, recreational, economic, spiritual, cultural and educational. Enhancing community resilience seems to offer a possible strategy which potentially reaches the most vulnerable children in the most sustainable and cost–effective manner.

CHAPTER 12
Guiding Principles for Programme Planning

THIS FINAL CHAPTER attempts to draw the threads of this book together by offering fourteen guiding principles which may be of value in future programme planning. First, however, three notes of caution will be offered.

First, empirical knowledge of the effects of conflict and displacement in children in a cross–cultural context is very limited. Few rigorous studies have been undertaken in the developing countries of the South, and our knowledge of the *long–term effects* is particularly weak. Inevitably, programmes have to be planned on certain assumptions about the psycho–social effects of war and displacement.

Second, there is also a lack of information about the impact of different approaches which respond to these psycho–social needs. The lack of impact evaluation of the programmes illustrated in this book was highlighted on Chapter 9.

Finally, we must all acknowledge that inappropriate approaches can actually make matters worse and inflict further damage on already vulnerable people. As Ressler et al.[104] remind us, "We must act on the current basis of what we hold to be true, but we are well advised to approach the topic of the psycho–social needs of children with openness and care, for with limited knowledge there is always the chance that harm rather than health will be perpetrated".

Rädda Barnen's experience, as exemplified in the case studies contained within this book, suggests that the following may be helpful in planning psycho–social programmes in the future:

Guiding Principles for Psycho–social Work with Children and Families Affected by War or Displacement

1. *Programmes should be based on people's own perceptions and definitions of their needs, problems, priorities and resources.* Planning should therefore be "bottom–up" in preference to the "top–down" approach espoused by some of those pursuing more western approaches[105].

2. *Programmes must be based on a thorough understanding of the culture.* It is vital that external agencies take the trouble to find out the precise manner in which people experience psycho–social distress, the meanings which they ascribe to their experiences, and the resources contained within the local culture which may contribute to healing and resilience. Religious beliefs, political affiliations and traditional beliefs and practices may all inform people's understandings of events and experiences.

3. In particular, programmes must acknowledge that in some situations the effects of conflict and displacement are *experienced in collective rather than individual terms*, in which case individualised responses are likely to be inappropriate.

4. *Psycho–social intervention should be regarded as an urgent priority* in refugee emergencies and conflict situations. Timely intervention at a very early stage may prove to be effective and cost–effective, but there may also be other "critical periods" for intervention such as post–conflict readjustment and return from exile.

5. It is vital to understand psycho–social reactions to conflict and displacement in the *context of the totality of people's experience*, and to avoid responding to just one small part of that totality. A *holistic approach* requires an understanding of the "person–in–family–in–community–in–wider–socio–political–context". It may be unhelpful to isolate psychological needs from the broader material, social, cultural, spiritual and educational needs of the people.

6. As far as possible, programmes should seek to avoid *isolating people who have been particularly affected by their experiences.* A broad focus based on the assumptions that entire populations have been

affected by their experiences may be preferable to the implicit labelling of individuals as particularly "traumatised" or "pschologically ill". *Social integration rather than segregation* should be encouraged.

7. Similarly, where possible programmes should be *integrated into existing structures* rather than providing specialised and separate facilities. An approach which emphasises *capacity–building* within existing organisations rather than the setting–up of separate and parallel organisations may be both effective and cost–effective.

8. Whatever approach is taken, the aim should be to maximise the *participation and empowerment of the people involved.* Wherever possible, programmes should aim to *build on the strengths and resources of individuals, groups and communities* rather than focusing on weaknesses. The active involvement of the community should be encouraged wherever possible.

9. A high priority should be given in any strategy to *support families.* Children should not be separated from their families unnecessarily, and steps to reunify children separated from their families should be taken as a matter of urgency. Pending family tracing and reunification, the provision of culturally appropriate care arrangements and support to *unaccompanied children* should also be accorded urgent priority.

10. Any approach should be founded on a *thorough understanding of child development* and the ways in which children's development is affected by conflict, violence and displacement. Children's needs for protection and security, the importance of daily routine and structure, and of play should all be recognised in programme planning.

11. Programmes need to *acknowledge the potential for stress and burnout in front–line workers* engaged in psycho–social work, and to take appropriate steps to provide supportive structures for them.

12. Agencies committed to achieving wider impact in their work need to *include elements of advocacy and public education* in their work in order to promote awareness of psycho–social issues, and influence policy and practice.

13. Organisations involved in psycho–social work have a

responsibility to document and evaluate their work in order to promote knowledge of psycho–social needs, develop new approaches and assess the impact of their work, and ensure that the results are disseminated as widely as possible. A greater emphasis on impact evaluation should also help agencies to determine, in advance, the appropriate stage at which their role can be concluded.

14. *The UN Convention on the Rights of the Child* should be a constant reference point for all agencies concerned with the psycho-social needs of children.

Conclusions

It is hoped that this book will make a small contribution to the development of knowledge and understanding in what is perhaps one of the most difficult and challenging areas of work for development agencies. Based on seven psycho–social programmes drawn from diverse parts of the world, Rädda Barnen's experience offers some important pointers for future developments in psycho–social work. In placing particular emphasis on community–based approaches, and in criticising some of the more Western therapeutic methods, it needs to be restated that the intention is not to assert that particular approaches are intrinsically and universally better or worse than others. Rather the aim has been to call attention to the need for approaches to be made relevant to the particular and unique social and cultural circumstances of each situation, and to avoid assumptions that approaches which are appropriate and relevant in one situation can be readily applied to another.

In the context of the developing countries of the South in which most conflicts have occurred in recent times, it does seem that more community–based approaches offer the most culturally sensitive and the most cost–effective means of reaching the large numbers of children and adults who have been adversely affected by their experiences of conflict or displacement. But that is not to say that a variety of different approaches cannot be built into a holistic, community–oriented strategy. Given the state of our present knowledge, diversity of approach and experimentation with new methods should be actively encouraged.

Whatever approaches seem to be appropriate to a particular situation, agencies need to take on board a central paradox: on the one hand, children need to be seen as vulnerable yet resilient, as having possibly overwhelming needs but also considerable personal resources. Refugee families may have been forced to abandon everything in the search for safety, yet they also display an unbreakable strength, an instinct and capacity for survival. Communities may have been torn apart by conflicts and disrupted by displacement, but may still contain the capacity for regeneration and for making available a wealth of resources to assist and support their most vulnerable members. The challenge for external agencies is to build on those capacities in a way which promotes child development, empowers people and encourages individual, family and community resilience.

PART II
The Case Studies

From Clinic to Community – the Work of Acisam in El Salvador

by David Tolfree

1. Introduction

ACISAM (Association for Training and Research in Mental Health) is an organisation which was born during the most critical years of political repression in El Salvador. A group of psychologists and students saw the need for assisting individuals whose lives were profoundly affected by oppression, imprisonment and torture inflicted on the civilian population by the government in the mid–1980s. Civil war had broken out at the beginning of the decade, between the guerillas of the FMLN, (a coalition of different groups), and the government army, heavily backed by the USA. Acisam is one of many NGOs which were closely associated with popular sectors and for this reason it was the object of pursuit by the Salvadoran armed forces. Under these circumstances, part of the work had to be carried out in a semi–clandestine way during the most critical period of political repression.

Initially, Acisam offered counselling and psychotherapy to individuals, support to people who sought refuge from the authorities, and assistance to people living in "marginalised communities" (temporary slum housing) in San Salvador. The primary focus of the organisation gradually shifted from *clinical inter-*

94

vention to *preventive approaches*, and following the peace agreement in 1992 it decided to concentrate its energies on *training and supporting volunteer Promoters* in village communities whose task was to offer a range of activities broadly described as mental health promotion. The task of training and supporting Promoters is undertaken by a cadre of Facilitators (currently eight), most of whom are professional psychologists, and who also actively participate in some community events, and in some cases undertake clinical work.

Acisam has chosen to work mainly with *rural communities* which have been *most affected by the civil war*. Many of these communities have had to face problems and issues regarding the resettlement of people who sought refuge outside of the country, or who were internally displaced, as well as many emotional, inter–personal, social and economic problems resulting directly from the war. Many of the communities where Acisam works are in areas controlled during the war by FMLN ("Liberated Zones"), which had assumed responsibility for providing various types of resource, including popular education and health services. In these areas, the level of community organisation had become high, but since the peace agreement, these communities have had to face the issues of the demobilisation of combatants and the widespread sense of disappointment with the limited change achieved as a result of the peace accord.

Although the needs of women and children have always been a high priority, Acisam has recently been aiming its work more specifically at *children and youth*, by training and deploying Young Promoters, and by working with Child and Youth Leaders. During the past year, Acisam has had to face the consequences of excessive dependence on Rädda Barnen for funding: in response to reduced funds it has had to contract its operation and is now successfully seeking to broaden its funding base.

2. Methodology

The following methodologies have been utilised in the compiling of this case study:

- a *review of available documentation*, including an evaluation of various NGOs in the region which are funded by Rädda Barnen, and a review of training materials
- viewing of a number of *video films* made by Acisam and illustrating various aspects of their work
- a series of *field visits to rural communities* accompanied by various members of Acisam's staff and Promoters, and by an interpreter. These included observation of training events and meetings for Promoters, Young Promoters and Child and Youth Leaders. Various group meetings for young people and families were observed, and semi–structured and informal discussions were held with Child and Youth Leaders, and also with community leaders.
- *group discussions and semi–structured interviews* with Facilitators and Promoters.
- *group and individual discussions* with Acisam staff
- *individual interviews* with key Rädda Barnen personnel
- The case study was *shared in draft* with staff within Acisam and amended in the light of comments received

The fieldwork was undertaken jointly with Birgitta Åberg, Rädda Barnen's Psycho-social Adviser, whose contribution to this case study is gratefully acknowledged.

3. Description of the Programme

3.1 The Effects of the War and the Implications of the Peace Agreement

Born in the years of extreme repression and violence, Acisam initially focused directly on the effects of war and violence, but increasingly the emphasis has shifted away from more clinical work to a broader concern not just with the aftermath of war but the totality of people's experiences in their local communities.

With regard to the more *direct effects of war*, Acisam has concerned itself with themes such as grief and loss, and especially with the widespread phenomenon of "frozen grief" experienced by people with difficulties in expressing their emotions. Significant in this are the suspicions and the lack of trust which exist in many communities, especially those which were very heterogenous politically and in which betrayal of individuals, including that by family, friends and neighbours, was common. Another factor inhibiting the expression of feelings was the set of values often associated with combatants: a machismo self–image and the need to avoid anything perceived as displaying "weakness".

Acisam has increasingly come to recognise that the main effects of war on people are not so much the classical symptoms of post–traumatic stress disorder, but the *indirect effects*: excessive use of drugs and alcohol (banned in the liberated areas during the war), increasing marital violence and child abuse, very authoritarian, militaristic attitudes, and a widespread feeling of despair and hopelessness. These problems figure significantly in the "community diagnoses" in which Promoters are involved – see paragraph 3.2 below. They particularly reflect people's disappointment at the outcome of the peace agreement and the sense that people had fought and died for a very limited result, and that many of the country's problems – poverty, corruption, inequality and injustice – remain relatively unchanged.

In the Liberated Zones, community organisation and a sense of solidarity and cohesion had been generally strong. Such factors are seen by Acisam staff as significant in enabling people to cope well with their reactions to war and violence. It is also their experience that combatants, despite what many experienced in the way of violence, torture and loss, often coped more effectively than the civilian population, who may be seen generally as the victims of the conflict rather than as active participants. On the other hand, in this post–war period, combatants who gained in self–esteem and public appreciation through the conflict now find themselves less valued, partly because of the widespread disappointment with the peace settlement.

Another effect of the war was that people were so preoccupied with their involvement with the conflict that there was little time for other things. Children themselves may have had little time for play, and parents may have had little time for their children apart from essential tasks. Encouraging playfulness, among children and parents, is an important aspect of Acisam's work.

A current trend within Acisam is to *focus more directly on children and youth*. They have found that not only are young people less affected than adults by the sense of hopelesness and despair, but also that they tend to be less polarised in their views. For these reasons children and young people can often be more readily mobilised to take action to transform their communities, and to work towards reconciliation.

3.2 The Role of the Promoters

Promoters are unpaid volunteers who work at grass–roots community level, usually motivated by religious factors or simply a desire to serve the community. The role of the Promoter is a *diverse one*, varying according to the characteristics and needs of the local community, the interests and abilities of the individual Promoter and the pattern of coordination and cooperation between local organisations. In some districts, the Acisam Promoters have a specific mental health role, whilst in others their work is part of an integrated health programme in which three organisations work together to train and support Promoters involved in the areas of general, dental and mental health.

Potential Promoters are *identified in the community*, a process which will usually involve the village committee and may actually involve a process of election. Though mainly young, usually they are people of established standing in the local community – e.g. popular teachers, village midwives, members of village committees, former FMLN combatants and so on. The majority are women, reflecting the particular concern with problems and issues being faced by both women and children, and their lesser involvement in income-generating work.

The mental health promotion work covers a *spectrum of activities*: at one end is the more "clinical" work which comprises tasks such as individual counselling (referred to in Acisam as "co–listening") and the setting up and supporting of self–help groups. At the other end of the spectrum are a wide range of community organisation activities which include, for example, organising sports and activities for young people; raising awareness of such issues as domestic violence, grief and loss, and alcoholism; giving talks to schools and other groups; adult education; organising cultural and recreational activities and celebrations; identifying local needs and negotiating for resources (e.g. wells and water pumps, road building, health facilities etc.). In addition, those Promoters who work within an integrated health framework undertake a wide range of health tasks which include, for example, treating minor ailments, advising on family planning and various health education tasks.

Although Promoters have a role and a range of tasks to perform in that role, Acisam's intention, in providing training and support, is also to introduce understanding of mental health issues into their broader work and life in the community. This is especially the case where Promoters also have other leadership roles such as that of popular educator or midwife. Although significant numbers of Promoters have given up that specific role over the years, it is hoped that they will continue to apply what they have learned from Acisam in other aspects of their work.

Acisam has developed the concept of the *"community self-diagnosis"* which involves Promoters working in a participative way within the local community to engage people in an exercise which examines the problems, resources and needs of the community and leads to an action plan which specifies what needs to be done to solve the problems identified, and to improve the overall health and well-being of the community.

3.3 Clinical Work

Acisam has gradually shifted its main emphasis away from direct work with individuals and groups towards a more holistic community-development focus. However, some clinical work does continue: some Facilitators, for example, conduct therapeutic

99

groups, and in some areas the work of Promoters has a particular emphasis on co–listening and facilitating the setting–up of self–help groups. They also use relaxation techniques, including a form of massage. However, Promoters are helped to acknowledge the limits of their clinical role and to refer cases to Facilitators which require more professional knowledge and skill.

A recurring theme is that of assisting individuals, groups and whole communities to deal with the mental health implications of the war. Helping people to deal appropriately with loss, grief, anger, fear and the other emotions associated with the war has been especially significant, sometimes described as "opening spaces" for people to express their emotions in an atmosphere of trust.

3.4 Promoter Training

Promoters undertake a pattern of training which varies according to the characteristics of the local situation and the particular interests and skills of the Facilitators who train them. In those areas where Promoters have an integrated health function, the training covers a wider range of health topics and is conducted jointly by the three NGOs involved. In other areas the focus is more specifically on mental health and community organisation issues. Core modules include the following:

- Community self-diagnosis
- Human beings
- Human life-cycle – including crisis intervention and grief
- Support techniques – including "co-listening" skills
- Organisation
- Addiction – including alcoholism

A style of training has been evolved that owes much to the popular education movement; it is *highly participatory* and designed to be relaxed and enjoyable, and a range of materials have been produced which have been aimed at people with either limited or no literacy skills. These utilise diagrams and comic–strips, and are designed to encourage reflection and questioning. Audio and video tapes, and large posters, are also used as educative tools.

The training methodologies used also serve to provide Promoters with skills in running workshops and in working in a participatory way. A variety of games and exercises are used, including role–play, drama, painting and other active and participatory approaches, all of which Promoters can then take into their work within their communities.

After receiving their basic training, Promoters receive on–going *training and support* which includes both visits from Facilitators and a pattern of meetings which are designed to help in the planning and reviewing of their work. Meetings are also held with Child and Youth Leaders, and both Facilitators and Promoters are involved in training workshops for these young people and in community events of various kinds.

3.5 Working with Young Promoters and Child and Youth Leaders

Acisam also deploys Young Promoters, who are usually older adolescents or young adults whose role is broadly similar to that of adult Promoters, with two exceptions: they do not undertake the more clinical work such as co–listening, and they have particular responsibility for reaching children and adolescents in their communities. By using sports and other recreational activities, music, dancing, video etc. as a means of gaining the interest of young people, they often then try to progress into other areas which may include, for example, workshop events (e.g. on topics such as alcoholism, health issues, sexuality, grief and loss etc.), and the development of modest economic activities. The aim with all of these activities is to help young people to be *organised and active and to take responsibility* within their local community for gaining resources and achieving change. Under their leadership, young people are also involved in community self–diagnosis. The compilation of village maps (which identify resources and resource gaps, community problems and so on) is a practical and enjoyable exercise which contributes to this process.

A relatively new departure is the identification of, and training and support to *child and youth leaders*. While there is considerable diversity within this concept, the basic idea is to identify young people with leadership potential to undertake a number of functions in respect of children and youth in the community, such as the organisation of sports and recreational activities, workshops on various topics and the promotion of awareness of mental health issues amongst the young (also with the intention of influencing adults) and the organising of community events. Another facet of their role appears to be that of providing a role model to other young people in communicating attitudes and values conducive to good mental health and community development. The role of the child leader is still evolving, and both Promoters and Facilitators play a role in training them and in supporting their work.

3.6 Coordination and Cooperation

In all areas there is an attempt to *integrate the work of Promoters with that of other NGOs*, many of whom also deploy Promoters, and with other local organisations, including the church and various social movements. In some areas, an approach is taken which integrates general, dental and mental health and this involves joint training and support by Acisam and two other health NGOs. In other areas, the coordination of NGOs at an institutional level is rather limited, but there is an expectation that Promoters cooperate with each other at the village level.

Coordination at Municipality level is also seen to be important. In many of the areas where Acisam works, especially the former Liberated Zones, political control is in the hands of various groups within the FMLN. Although it rarely works well, this makes closer coordination possible, and where it is effective the impact of the work of the Promoters is greater.

However, since the peace agreement, there has been a gradual attempt for Acisam to be seen as more independent of political parties, and attempts are now being made to *coordinate with both the government and with Municipalities not controlled by FMLN* factions.

3.7 Broader Training and Publicity Work

An important aspect of Acisam's work consists of what they describe as "communications". This includes the production of videos on diverse mental health topics (both for training purposes and for television transmission to the general public), designing and running training courses and seminars, the production of a journal on mental health issues, and a book has also been produced in conjunction with psychologists in the region. Through these means they have attempted to influence public opinion, promote awareness of mental health issues and encourage the development of non–traditional approaches.

3.8 Evaluation

In every aspect of their work, evaluation is seen as an important component: for example, the regular meetings between Promoters and Facilitators aim to evaluate the work of the previous period as well as to plan for the next one, and normally end with an evaluation of the meeting. Similarly, workshops include an element of evaluation by the participants, using various games and exercises as a means of doing so, as well as verbal feedback.

In terms of evaluating the overall impact of the work, it has been acknowledged that measuring such things as self esteem and community participation is intrinsically difficult, and Acisam is currently working on the task of developing indicators that will help them to evaluate the impact of their work in local communities.

4. Discussion and Analysis

4.1 Conceptualisations of Health

Acisam pursues an *integrative model of health* that is described as "the dynamic product of a satisfactory interrelationship process between biological and psychological factors of the people and their socio-economic, cultural and ecological environment, which contributes to the collective as well as individual development"[1]. The change in the organisation's emphasis in recent years reflects a shift from *treating psychological problems*, to mental health *prevention* and to more holistic *promotion* within local communities.

Nevertheless, Acisam have retained the language of *health and mental health* in their work despite the generally rather negative connotations of mental health in the minds of most Salvadoreans. The tendency is to associate the concept with mental illness and with madness, rather than the overall, holistic approach which the above definition makes clear. Despite the flexibility of Acisam's approach, their continuing reference points in health, and more specifically in mental health, may serve to limit their work in local communities.

On the other hand, Acisam's approach is highly significant in moving away from *individualised concepts of mental health* and recognising, for example, the importance of identifying the effects of war in community terms. A striking example of this was found in one village which, every year, celebrates the return of its people from exile in Honduras[2]. Previously an individualistic and fragmented community, this village achieved a strong sense of community and a high level of community organisation as a result of traumatic experiences in the war and subsequent experience of exile. An Acisam Promoter suggested ways in which the community might celebrate their return, but the village committee decided on the idea of re–enacting the circumstances leading to flight into exile. This re–enactment, which involved large numbers of adults and children, both preserved a highly significant part of the village history, and also served therapeutic purposes in encouraging people to talk about these traumatic events *within the context of the whole community sharing memories together*. Significantly, this village seemed relatively free from problems such as drug and alcohol abuse, and it seems likely that the sense of community solidarity is an important reason for this.

An interesting feature of Acisam's experience is that it is not found to be useful to respond to the reactions of individuals and communities to their experiences of war and conflict in isolation from other issues being faced in rural communities. The specific effects of conflict and violence, and the implications of the peace accord are inextricably intertwined, making it necessary to *respond to the totality of people's experiences* and not to any one particular aspect of those experiences.

4.2 Professional Orientation

Perhaps rather surprisingly, and despite the move towards a broad, community–development approach to their work, the *dominant profession within Acisam remains that of psychology*, with 7 out of 8 Facilitators coming from a background in that discipline. However, staff are chosen more for their personal qualities and experience than their professional background, and Facilitators have clearly had to adapt and change their approach as the philosophy of Acisam has evolved. One remaining weakness, however, is perhaps that the *economic* determinants of health continue not to be emphasised very strongly in their work.

With the passage of time, and as the need to help people with regard to the direct effects of war recedes (grief, loss, fear and the specific problems associated with combatants reintegrating into civilian life), it seems likely that Acisam will need to recruit staff with a broader range of knowledge and skills in community development to supplement and complement the personal resources of their psychologists. This trend will, perhaps, be accompanied by a decreased emphasis on such problem areas as grief and loss, drug and alcohol abuse, inter–personal violence etc., and an increasing emphasis on poverty and the need for broad economic, educational, social and community development. The language of human development, and of community development, may become more useful than that of health and of mental health.

4.3 Participation

One vital aspect of Acisam's ideology is the notion of *participation*, based on the belief derived from the popular education movement, that people can transform both themselves and their environment if given the opportunity to identify and develop their own competence, and their personal and comunity resources. Hence the importance of *horizontal relationships* between people, based on mutual trust and respect, and the acknowledgement that people are resourceful and that learning and growth can emerge from the process of reflecting on their own experience. Acisam's willingness to recruit as Promoters, people without literacy skills is a tangible illustration of Acisam's belief that ordinary people can transform their communities. The educational approach and the materials produced are an impressive demonstration of how the principle of participation can be fully realised in a practical and non–patronising way.

4.4 Coverage and Affordability

Acisam's strategy – like that of many other NGOs in the region – aims to *achieve maximum coverage and cost–effectiveness*. The approach can be described as an attempt to achieve widespread impact by diffusing psychological knowledge and understandings into local communities through the deployment of volunteer Promoters. By this means the costs of the programme are relatively low, while strenuous attempts are made to maintain high standards largely through the work done by Facilitators to train, support and supervise the Promoters. A dilemma currently being faced, however, is how to maintain the commitment of Promoters without offering any financial rewards. One option currently being considered is to involve Promoters in various cooperatives or other forms of income–generating activity. A significant result of this may be an increasing emphasis on the importance of economic development in local communities.

Other developments being considered as a means of increasing coverage and cost–effectiveness include the possibility of *using more experienced Promoters as "Multipliers"*. This would involve them in training and supporting other Promoters, thereby extending further the existing "cascade" approach to training and support. This would then free the Facilitators to begin work in new areas of the country. Another possibility is to develop the idea of *Associates*, who would work on a voluntary basis.

4.5 Coordination with Other Structures

A vital aspect of Acisam's attempt to achieve maximum and widespread impact of their work is the need for *coordination with local structures*. Integration with village committees and with Municipal authorities (where this is possible), coordination with other NGOs (especially those which also deploy Promoters), liaison with churches and coordination with other local organisations are all seen as vital. The increasing emphasis on working with the Government (considered unthinkable until comparatively recently) is an important aspect of maximising their influence and impact. However, coordination and cooperation with some key individuals within local communities is less strong. Traditional healers, for example, do play an important part in responding to people's personal problems, but there is no self–conscious attempt to work with them at local level.

The fact that Acisam has been closely associated with the FMLN has both positive and negative consequences: particularly in the former Liberated Zones, Acisam has been able to build up trust more readily and to work extremely closely with local authorities. On the other hand, because Acisam is identified with the FMLN, working in areas where the FMLN is less strong can be more problematic.

Many communities in El Salvador are very polarised politically, and the lack of trust and the fear of betrayal continue to be extremely strong in many of them. The need for *community reconciliation* is a very real one, but because Acisam is identified with a political movement, this may be a particularly difficult area to achieve impact. It was significant that one group of Promoters interviewed for the compilation of this case study saw the divisions and distrust within their community as a factor which made their work difficult, rather than as a potentially important focus for their work. A major challenge for Acisam in the future is to find ways of working towards community reconciliation. It is important for it to be seen as having a concern with and for all sections of local communities, but without, however, abandoning the ideological basis of their work, i.e. a concern for justice and equality, the need for reforms which will benefit the poorer sections of society, and a commitment to human rights and children's rights.

5. Conclusions

Perhaps one of the most remarkable features of Acisam has been its ability to adapt as circumstances within El Salvador have changed: from a concern with the immediate *psychological effects of war*, to the *problems associated with peace*. From a largely clinical perspective, it has moved to prevention and then to promotion of mental health as its major focus. From a highly political organisation, it has had to adjust to becoming an NGO with a role with all sectors of society, with community reconciliation as an important and challenging task. The willingness to continually review both its conceptual framework and its methods of work should place the organisation in a strong position to use the present period of political transition as a platform for change, and to continue to grow and develop in response to the changes within Salvadorean society.

A Special Form of Social Integration – the Work of Hi Neighbour in Yugoslavia

by David Tolfree

1. Background and Introduction

The conflict in the former Yugoslavia began in 1990 when parts of the Federation attempted to secede. The most serious and widespread fighting occurred in Bosnia–Hercegovina, and though what remained of the Federal Republic of Yugoslavia (Serbia and Monenegro) had little direct involvement in the fighting, they were hosts to large numbers of refugees, mainly from Bosnia–Hercegovina. Though the majority of refugees were living with host families, significant numbers were housed in Collective Centres. The economic sanctions imposed by the UN had a devastating effect on the economy which exacerbated further the widespread feeling of despair which affected the whole population.

Hi Neighbour[3] has its roots in events in 1992 when a group of developmental psychologists, based in the University of Belgrade in Serbia, under the leadership of Vesna Ognjenović, became concerned about the effects of war on all children in the former Yugoslavia, and in particular at the issues facing the growing number of children and families seeking refuge in the Federal Republic (FRY).

As a prelude to planning a programme, they undertook some work with children attending pre–schools in order to assess the impact of war on children generally – not specifically refugee children or those who had direct experience of the war. The results were startling: free drawings and observations of children's play indicated a number of particularly striking factors:

- a *preoccupation with war* – sometimes almost an obsession with themes connected with the war
- a dramatic effect on the *colours used by children* in their drawings, including such symbolic use of colour as flowers and suns coloured black and a generally sombre tone to many drawings
- in their play, children displayed, in an obsessive manner, their *reactions* to war, but their playing tended to be rigid and lacked the vital ingredient of normal play which is the *elaboration* of their experience and not merely reactions to it
- children's play also demonstrated an increased component of *aggression*
- children perceived the end of the war in terms such as *"extermination" rather than reconciliation*, peace–making or conflict–resolution, suggesting that adults have not given children divergent ways of thinking about the war and the possible ways in which the conflict might be resolved.

When they came into closer contact with children in the Collective Centres (usually large institutional buildings), what they observed was even more alarming: They found that many children were simply *unable to play*, many having experienced violence, sudden uprootedness and separation, as well as facing an uncertain future in a very constraining living environment. They also found that many parents (mainly mothers) displayed a *reduced level of parental competence* as a result of their experiences. Not infrequently they actually *inhibited the expression of emotion* by their children – indeed children sometimes adopted "parenting" roles vis à vis their parents, caring for them and sometimes attempting to "protect" their mothers from emotional expression. They also found that adults in particular were very isolated, experiencing difficulties in making social contacts outside of the Centres.

They also found that refugees felt a loss of a sense of individuality and personal identity. Experiencing repeated moves as refugees, finding that people did not know their names, or used inappropriate nicknames, added to the problem. Moreover, because of the loss of their homes and the experience of displacement, compounded by the lack of privacy and permanence in the Collective Centres, the lack of, and need for, a sense of "personal space" was striking.

When it came to developing their methodology, Hi Neighbour had no model to build on, though they did have experience of running workshop groups with children, and decided to develop this approach, and the methodology grew and evolved with experience. The central part of the programme consists of *workshop groups*, run in Collective Centres usually, on a weekly basis.

Initially working entirely as part–time *volunteers*, in 1994 they registered themselves as an NGO and were successful in securing funding from UNHCR and later from Rädda Barnen. This enabled them to expand the programme, and new influxes of refugees in September and October 1995 prompted further expansion. The programme now encompasses some 44 Collective Centres, offering a total of about 400 workshop groups per month. However, they continue to deploy psychologists on a *part–time, minimally paid basis* ("semi–volunteers"), their main expenses being office space rental , transport and workshop materials.

More recently they have expanded their work into a programme of *"social integration"* designed to provide the refugees with opportunities for social interaction and purposeful activities both within the Centres and with people outside. They have also developed a joint project with International Rescue Committee to set up centres primarily for refugees in host families, which offer counselling and advice, various workshop group activities, a range of educational and cultural activities and a "drop–in" facility. This development will not, however, be discussed in any detail in this case study, the main focus of which is on the workshop groups.

Despite the recent growth in the organisation, it still has the positive characteristics of a *small organisation* – it is informal, non–bureaucratic and people–oriented. A group of people in the Belgrade office act as a management group which also takes responsibility for the development and supervision of other teams of psychologists working in other parts of the FRY.

The work of Hi Neighbour is founded on the work of the Russian developmental psychologist Lev Vygotsky. Because of the theoretically complex basis of the work, an account of its theoretical foundations is included as an appendix to this case study.

2. Methodologies Used in Compiling this Case Study

In compiling this case study, the following were the main methodologies used:

- *perusal of project documents* and articles written by project staff
- *participant observation of workshop groups*, including those for children, for adolescents, for adults and a joint workshop for all age–groups
- *semi–structured group and individual interviews* with people working for Hi Neighbour
- *informal discussion with refugees* participating in the programme
- *attendance at a weekly review/planning meeting* of the Belgrade team of psychologists
- *attendance at the project's management committee*
- The case study was *shared in draft* with staff within Hi Neighbour and amended in the light of comments received

3. Description of the Programme

3.1 The Workshops – Rationale, Methods and Topics

The project offers a regular pattern of workshop groups in the Collective Centres in which it has chosen to work. Two or more psychologists are deployed in each group, and typically a group for children, one for adolescents and one for adults operate concurrently, with periodic joint workshops for all ages. The groups are open, refugees are free to join and leave at will, and an important aspect of their work is the wish for the workshop to reflect realities of life within the Centres.

Workshop sizes vary greatly, from 2 or 3 people to as many as 60 attending a joint workshop event. Each workshop group, which takes up to about two hours, usually involves a wide variety of different activities. They usually begin in a large circle, with the theme of personal names, personal signs and faces which serve to validate individuals and emphasise personal identity and individuality. Workshops also end with participants in a large circle with some sort of experience which, often in a ritual–like manner, draws the workshop to a conclusion. The workshops are usually preceded by a period of informal interaction, over coffee with the refugees: part of Hi Neighbour's aim is befriending, and on some occasions the psychologists will assist the refugees with practical tasks such as harvesting, preparing meals or undertaking maintenance work in the Centres.

The whole approach is based on the belief that all refugees are deeply affected by their experience, but by avoiding labelling people as "traumatised" or as "having problems", they are able to work in a way that *builds on people's strengths* rather than weakness. No attempt is made to "solve" problems or to suggest action which they can take. Rather the aim is to provide a *special form of social interaction* and the "*tools*" with which people themselves can discover and build on their own and each other's personal resources.

Media such as drawing and painting, clay modelling, story telling and performing, movement and human sculpting, creative and expressive games and exercises all facilitate individual and group expression and exploration of the reality they are in and its emotional significance for them. One particularly important medium is that of "performances"; these comprise role–played enactments which are usually minimally prepared and performed by small groups in front of the whole workshop. By such means, children (and sometimes adults) can creatively and imaginatively work on issues which they select.

There are some obvious differences between workshops for children and adults. The latter, for example, rely rather more on discussion and less on activities, though drawing and a range of other media are used. Sometimes the workshops for children, for adolescents and for adults in the same Collective Centre will pursue the same theme, sometimes sharing what they have done with each other at the end of the workshop.

Workshop groups are planned in advance. The project has developed a large battery of workshop *"scripts"* which are used flexibly in order to provide opportunities for responding to themes and issues which emerge in the workshops. These scripts are grouped in "pools" of topics, and usually a "pool" of 3 or 4 workshops pursue one particular theme, often ending in a joint workshop group for all age groups together.

These scripts are very diverse: some reflect such themes as feelings, faces and self–expression, identity, self–esteem, personal space etc. in a way which provides opportunities for participants to use those experiences as they find appropriate, without necessarily being directed towards particularly poignant issues facing them. Special workshops are used as a means of celebrating birthdays or other special events.

Other scripts reflect, more immediately, the *themes and issues which are particularly pertinent to refugees*: for example, the "pool" of workshops on "faces" includes a workshop entitled "faces I haven't seen for a long time but would like to see", and the pool on the theme of "together" includes a workshop on "the home we share together". New workshops are devised around particular issues which emerge within the Collective Centre, or which refugees themselves request. One example is a recent request for a workshop on the emotive issue of "revenge".

In general, the preferred approach is to use workshops as a means of enabling the participants to introduce whatever issues they choose. A particularly striking example which was recorded on video was a workshop with the very open title of "let's make a performance" which was used in a Collective Centre in which the refugees were faced with the prospect of having to move to another Centre. Children dressed up and used face paints, and divided into groups to make and then enact a story. One group performed a story on the highly symbolic theme of "a circus comes to town", while another performed a complex story around the themes of killing and revenge.

3.2 "The Prolonged Workshop Effect"

As already indicated, the workshop groups are open, both in the sense that anybody may attend them, with no long–term commitment required, and also in the sense that people can join and leave the group session. In contrast with more traditional therapeutic groups, this openness is designed to enable the work-shops to reflect the issues actually being faced in the *real–life world* of the Collective Centre, rather than removing participants from that context into a more artificially–constituted group.

The "prolonged workshop effect" is a way of describing the intended outcome of the workshops in helping refugees to change the pattern of interaction among themselves – for example, in encouraging the expression of feelings, in achieving a high level of caring and tolerance, in developing non–violent means of resolving conflict. One example was experienced during the fieldwork for this case study when, during a period of informal interaction before the workshops started, a group of mainly older women began, quite naturally, to share memories and feelings derived from their own painful experiences. There was some tearfulness and laughter, all in an atmosphere of quiet reflection, mutual care and support.

The leaders strive to help the participants to *actively work on the here–and–now issues* facing them: this is particularly the case in workshops for adults. This was vividly demonstrated in a workshop in a Collective Centre for recently arrived refugees, in which, despite many expressions of despair and hopelessness, a large group of participants mobilised energy to actually deal with some of the current problems and frustrations they were facing, culminating in decisions about concrete actions that some of them resolved to take.

3.3 Workshop Leadership

There are always at least two psychologists in each group, one taking the main leadership role, but this changes from one workshop session to another. The main leader has a role in facilitating the workshop, following the script (and departing from it where it seems appropriate). In contrast to the approach more typical of clinical psychology, the leaders do not, in general, offer interpretations or evaluative comments on what the participants contribute. They tend to ask "what?" and "how?" questions, but not "why" questions, seeing it as their role to *help the participants to raise questions themselves* and then *seek appropriate responses* rather than posing direct questions or offering possible answers. Again in contrast to clinical approaches, strong individual relationships between the leaders and the workshop members are not seen as important, hence the possibility of changes in leadership which do not impede the progress of the groups.

In the workshop groups observed in the preparation of this case study, the leaders appeared to *value* of all contributions without being *evaluative*. The psychologists other than the formal leader took part as participants, modelling appropriate behaviour (e.g by expressing feelings and offering support) as well as adopting a more formal leadership in sub–group activities.

3.4 Social Interaction Programmes

While it was the experience of Hi Neighbour that the Workshops had a significant impact on the quality of social interaction within the Collective Centres where they worked, many refugees experienced problems and anxieties in moving away from the safety and isolation of the Centres and engaging in social interaction with people in the local community. This led to the initiation of a range of activities designed to *improve the interaction between refugees and people outside the Centres*. This had several components:

- *meetings with refugees* from other Collective Centres were arranged
- a range of *outings and cultural visits* were arranged – e.g. museum

and theatre visits, outings to Belgrade. In addition, writers, poets etc. were encouraged to visit the Centres to offer cultural activities with refugees

- refugees were encouraged to *act as hosts* to other people such as the parents of local children attending the pre–school

In such activities, the role of Hi Neighbour has been to encourage the refugees themselves to articulate their own wishes and needs and then respond by providing resources – transport, funds and personnel where needed.

In addition, refugees requested opportunities for taking part in *traditional activities* such as craftwork. The project responded by deploying an artist to design clothes and other craft items, provide materials, train refugees to train others in traditional skills and to begin to find ways of marketing the goods produced so as to provide a modest income for refugees. This provided not only a range of purposeful activities for adult refugees, mainly women, but also brought them into closer interaction with each other: this social function was considered to be as important as the activity and the modest material gains resulting from it. But all three benefits result in *enhancing their sense of self–esteem and self–respect.*

3.5 Review and Evaluation

Three approaches have been taken in reviewing and evaluating Hi Neighbour's work. First, on a weekly basis, each team of psychologists meets to *review the previous week's workshops* and *plan the next.* The psychologists working together in a particular workshop also meet to complete a comprehensive recording format, which provides a structure for discussing and evaluating each workshop and which encourages analytical reflection on a week–by–week basis. These meetings provide opportunities for the critical and self–critical examination of their work, and for planning and replanning future workshops. The process also feeds into the wider development of the project, for example by identifying the need for new workshop topics.

A second approach to evaluation is the *more formal evaluation* (perhaps more appropriately described as review), undertaken by psychologists in the Belgrade office in respect of each of the other teams on a six–monthly basis. Three teams, plus members of the Belgrade team, sit down together, and first identify the strengths in the teams, and then their problems and weaknesses. This then generally broadens out into a discussion of steps which need to be taken to develop each team's work and to address any problem areas identified.

Third, a few early attempts have been made to *evaluate the impact* of the workshops on the participants, for example by using sentence completion and drawing exercises, and also rating scales and questionnaires with participants. By these means they have satisfied themselves about the impact of their work on child development. However, project staff also describe their work, like human development, as a "never–ending process". Rather than working towards some pre–determined outcomes, the work is seen as needing to continue for as long as the refugees remain. Refugees leave, new ones arrive in the Centres, and new issues emerge; their role in offering friendship is also seen as a long–term need. By its nature, the work is about social interaction rather than attempting to solve particular problems.

4. Discussion and Analysis

4.1 Originality and Innovation

The work of Hi Neighbour comprises a highly original model which has been devised on the basis of the identified needs of the refugees and the particular theoretical orientation of the psychology staff involved in the project.

It operates on a *multiplicity of levels*: at a basic level it provides simple friendship, and cultural and recreational activities which are valuable for their own sake. At another level it offers a conceptually complex approach to child and human development which calls for very precise, purposeful and sophisticated work but which, in practice is implemented in a relaxed, friendly, non–confrontational manner. Technical terms are consistently avoided within the workshops, yet their work is defined and analysed by reference to a theoretically coherent framework. The work is highly professional yet, at the same time, many of the typical characteristics of professional relationships are avoided, such as professional distance and inter–personal formality. The willingness of the psychologists to work within the real–life situation of the Centres rather than withdrawing people into a "special" group situation is also a hall-mark of their work.

4.2 Openness and Inclusiveness

One of the most startling aspects of Hi Neighbour's work is that it has, as its starting point, two important statements about refugees. First, all refugees are assumed to have been psychologically affected by their experiences of violence, disruption and displacement, and rather than defining people's reactions to such events as "traumatising" they prefer to perceive them as *ordinary people in difficult life situations*".

Second, the model avoids the terminology of healing and therapy: rather the approach is firmly based on a *developmental perspective* which views human beings as having capacities and personal resources to identify issues they need to work on, and to deal with these themselves. By avoiding the typical stereotype of the refugee as helpless and passive, they find ways in which the tremendous strengths and resources contained within the refugee community can be harnessed and utilised. By avoiding terms which label people as "traumatised" or "pathological", they work with their strengths rather than on their weaknesses.

The open nature of the workshop groups enables the psychologists to enter the "life space" of the Collective Centres and become involved with the totality of the social environment of the refugees and whatever issues are around for them. In this sense, the workshops are like a *microcosm of the whole centre* with the aim that the "prolonged workshop effect" will provide refugees with some tools with which to continue to work on obstacles to their personal development.

The openness of the groups means that no stigma is attached to participation. But it is signficant that individuals who have been profoundly affected by their experiences are not only free to join in, but are also accepted as valuable members of the group. One of the groups observed in compiling this case study included a woman who described herself as "having psychological problems". She was accepted fully into the group, was able to contribute and, it appears, drew strength from it. There is, however, no claim that severely traumatised people are "treated" in the workshops, and referrals to more specialised facilities are encouraged where appropriate.

It was clear that *people with profound psychological problems were able to use the opportunities of the workshops to express feelings, face difficult experiences and issues*, and moreover to contribute to the development of other people. This is seen to have a beneficial impact on their sense of well–being.

4.3 Gender Issues

Some of the workshops observed in compiling this case study had a marked *gender imbalance*, with girls and women very much in the majority, although this is not an invariable characteristic. The un-der–representation of younger men in the centres is only a partial explanation for this phenomenon.

One notable exception to this was a very large workshop for newly arrived refugees in which there was a significant male repre-sentation, and in which a number of men were highly influential in contributing their psychological strength and personal resources. By contrast, in another Collective Centre, no men attended the group for adults, and most of the children attending their workshop were girls. Many of the older women in this centre were highly committed to the workshops, contributing freely from their own experiences of war 50 years ago, but adding their great wisdom and life experience.

The model being pursued lays great emphasis on the need for and value of utilising the *potentiality of the whole interactive field* in the

Centres. Clearly a challenge for the future lies in finding ways of involving men to a greater extent than occurs in some of the workshops, and in enabling them to become more active players in the programme. In the context of the many fatherless families in the Centres, it seems important to enable them to contibute more fully to the development of the children.

4.4 Sustainability and Replicability

The open–ended nature of the workshop groups, and the need to deploy significant numbers of qualified and experienced professional psychologists raises questions about the long–term sustainability and affordability of the programme, and its replicability in situations where such skilled human resources might not be available.

Hi Neighbour ensures the affordability of its programme by virtue of deploying psychologists on a *semi–volunteer basis* – i.e. they are paid only symbolic amounts, and it is clear that if funding were to become a serious problem the majority would be willing to continue to work on an unpaid basis.

Perhaps it is partly because of this that there appears to be within the project an unwillingness to consider working other than on this open–ended and potentially long–term basis. For example, the concept of the "prolonged workshop effect" has not been extended into a consideration of identifying a point at which the workshops could be discontinued. It might be possible to devise a set of indicators which would help determine that patterns of social interaction within the Centres have developed to a point where the workshops are no longer needed. Most of the *evaluation* work within the project focuses on critically examining the *process* rather than the *outcome* of their work.

4.5 The Impact of Early Intervention

The fieldwork for this case study was undertaken at a stage when large numbers of refugees had recently arrived, especially from Krajina. One issue to emerge from Hi Neighbour's work is that it has highlighted the advantages of working with refugees at this early and critical stage rather than months or years after the refugees arrive.

Although it is dangerous to generalise from specific experience, it was very striking that Hi Neighbour's work with newly arrived refugees seemed to be characterised by the release of a great deal of *creative energy* among the refugees, despite the exceptionally difficult circumstances they had experienced and the current stresses and privations they were faced with. Some Collective Centres have a mixture of recent arrivals and more long–standing refugees. One psychologist working in such a context described the emotions of the more recently arrived refugees as "much more on the surface". It was found that there is often a greater capacity for self–expression, especially regarding negative emotions such as anger and horror.

5. Conclusions

Hi Neighbour's work is a highly original approach developed in response to local circumstances. In part, the approach is based on perceptions of the circumstances of the refugees, including the belief that all have been psychologically affected by their experiences of war and displacement, and the evidence of the impact on children derived from their research.

The model also reflects the drive and commitment of a group of psychologist who felt the need to develop an appropriate response, coupled with their particular theoretical orientation which emphasised strengths rather than weaknesses, the capacity for growth and development rather than a propensity for despair, dependence and depression. The resulting methodology provides a context for a special form of social interaction and a set of "tools" which enable refugees to set their own agendas and work purposefully on the many obstacles to their own growth and development, drawing primarily on the resources and strengths contained within the refugee community.

Although this programme is built on a particular child development framework rather than specifically pursuing the concept of *resilience*, the two approaches have much in common.

The idea of facilitating social interaction, of enabling young people to develop cognitive, social and emotional competence, and of promoting self–esteem and a sense of mastery over difficult life experiences – all these objectives have much in common with programmes aimed as enhancing resilience. Both have as their starting point the belief that people have a wealth of personal resources to bring to bear on even overwhelming difficulties. The task is to support these capacities rather than to provide "treatment".

In particular, the Hi Neighbour approach builds on the great capacity of children for creative and imaginative play, through which difficult issues can be explored, feelings can be expressed and a sense of hope can be found despite the extreme difficulties facing them.

The following story was written by a group of children in a workshop called "my personal sign":

> In the field of flowers a boy was wandering. He was holding tight to his heart a boomerang of kindness, uncertain what would happen to his boomerang if people receive it. Would it come back to him as boomerangs always do? The boy took a chance. He threw his boomerang of kindness to people. Kindness went all the way to the sun and was coming back at people together with sunshine. The boy was looking into the blue sky and waiting.
>
> His boomerang came back to him as boomerangs always do. Kindness of people was with him mingling with sunshine around his heart. The boy was certain now, and for ever, that boomerangs do come back to the one that sends it to the others.

This story is significant not just because of the extraordinarily powerful imagery, but because it resulted from the creative imagination of children. Here was a group of children surrounded by the horrors of a war which adults had imposed on their lives, but despite everything they were still able to perceive their own, and other people's capacity for kindness and peace.

Appendix: Theoretical Foundations of Hi Neighbour's Work

The Hi Neighbour Programme is founded particularly on the work of the Russian psychologist, *Lev Vygotsky*. He viewed the *entire social network* of the growing child as having a crucial impact on child development. Not only parents, but other adults such as relatives, neighbours, pre–school and school teachers, etc. All have an important role in the child's cognitive and emotional development. He also saw a particular significance in *social interaction with other children* and emphasised the role of the peer group in promoting child development by offering a particular quality of stimulation. Hi Neighbour has developed this approach further in seeing the potential for *children promoting change in adults*.

Vygotsky and his followers saw particular importance in the child's *creative imagination*, and in the development of *imaginative play*, reflecting the limitations of language in children, though cognitive development, through a growing capacity for conceptual thinking, becomes increasingly important as the child develops. According to Vygotsky, play is "not simply a recollection of past experience, but a creative reworking that combines impressions and constructs from them new realities addressing the needs of the child"[4].

He used the term *"zone of proximal development"* to describe the gap between what the child can accomplish him/her self and what can be accomplished through interacting with more competent others (adults or older children). This led him to emphasise the importance of providing children with a form of assistance that goes slightly beyond the child's present competence by building on existing abilities rather than directly teaching new behaviours. Post–Vygotskians have used the term "assymetry" to describe a form of interaction with children which promotes development in this way, for example by stimulating new and divergent ways of thinking rather than merely reacting to what the child is saying or doing, or teaching new ideas.

Hi Neighbour uses the workshop medium as an opportunity for children to use play, drawings, games and various activities as a means of becoming more aware of themselves and their feelings, expressing themselves, and exploring whatever issues they themselves choose to examine. Workshop leaders try to adopt "assymetical" ways of interacting with children but also use other members of the groups to promote development in the children. Workshops involving children and adults together, for example, open up possibilities of children being influenced by other adults (e.g. elderly refugees) and, significantly, provide opportunities for children to influence the personal development of adults – through, for example, their greater spontaneity in expressing emotions and engaging in imaginative play, which are particularly significant in the light of the "emotional frozenness" which has been observed in many parents.

Promoting Community Healing Networks: the Work of the National Children and Violence Trust, South Africa

by Dr. Martha Tshitshi Mbatha

1. Introduction and Background to the Project

The National Children and Violence Trust (NCVT) is a non–government organisation based in Johannesburg. It was founded in 1990 by its current Honorary Director, Mrs Hlengiwe Mkhize who, during the 1980s came into contact with many young victims of violence when they came to seek the counselling services from her office.

The period between the late eighties and the early nineties was marked by an escalation of political violence in South Africa. The political strategy for bringing about the downfall of the National Party Government entailed putting children in the forefront of direct action. Young people were the victims of state–initiated violence, and were both the victims and the perpetrators of factional violence. Domestic violence, sexual violence and school–based violence were all indicative of the "cycle of violence" which had developed.

At this time, the founder was working as a lecturer at the University of Witwatersrand's Department of Psychology. As she herself explains the situation at that time:

"I was concerned about the incidence of political violence which often resulted in loss of lives, injuries, displacement of households, trauma, impoverishment and disorganisation of family and community life. As a result of a host of factors related to apartheid laws, black communities could not access mental health services. The majority of both the government and private services were situated in areas previously reserved for whites. Some of these services were inappropriate to black South Africans since the majority of service providers were white people with limited understanding of black people's cultural meanings of violence and processes of psychological healing. Moreover, mental health services were, and are still unaffordable to the disadvantaged communities".

The founder's initial response was to offer individual consultations and counselling to these victims of violence, but as the numbers of people seeking her assistance increased, she realised that a different approach was needed. Despite the lack of professional counsellors in the black neighbourhoods she realised that communities were not "empty terrains" and that a variety of approaches would be needed in order to work in a more neighbourhood–based way, utilising people from within those communities. She accepted such a challenge with enthusiasm and pioneered the project now called the National Children and Violence Trust. Initially relying entirely on part–time psychologists, it now has its own staff team.

The main sponsor of the project has been Rädda Barnen, with other organisations also playing a part. NCVT is governed by a Board of Trustees: in addition to the honorary Director, the staff team comprises the Executive Director, National Coordinator,

Programme Supervisor, Lead Trainer, Administrative Secretary and Network Coordinators located at the various networks of the project. The founder has now become its Honorary Director.

The main objective of this case study is to describe and discuss the development of the project during the apartheid era, and for this reason more recent developments are not discussed in detail.

2. Methodologies Used in Compiling the Case Study

In the process of conducting the case study, the following data collection methods were used:

- *Observation* of project activities, and participant observation in training workshops
- *Review of project documentation*, including annual reports, papers presented by the Director, evaluation reports, workshop programmes and case reports of clients counselled
- *Semi–structured interviews* with project staff and members of community–based networks
- *Viewing of videotapes* on the project
- the case study was *shown to project staff* and amended in the light of comments received.

3. The Assumptions and Philosophy of the Project

The NCVT aims at meeting the needs of children and families affected by violence, and operates on the basis of the following assumptions:

- Children experience *multiple forms of violence*, which manifest themselves in aggression which characterises South African society
- There is an *inter–relationship between political and other forms of violence*

- Since the consequences of apartheid will remain for many years to come, there is a *need for activities and organisations that address issues relating to violence*

The National Children and Violence Trust operates under the following guiding principles:
- the delivery of *accessible programmes and services*
- *empowerment* of individuals, families, organisations and communities
- *appropriateness* of interventions in a societal context
- *culturally sensitive* interventions and the development of *indigenous* models of intervention
- *innovation* – the development of new and unconventional strategies for tackling the problems of violence against children and families
- *holism* and the utilisation of multi–disciplinary approaches
- *effectiveness* in reaching those in need

4. Understanding the Impact of Violence and Developing Culturally Appropriate Responses

A number of concepts are central to the work of the NCVT. Taking an Eriksonian perspective, they have closely examined the ways in which children's development is affected by experiences of violence. Equally important has been the attempt to integrate within this framework indigenous knowledge and practices, including traditional children's games, and to use approaches which draw on these practices.

4.1 The Impact of Violence on Child Development

In seeking to develop understanding of the impact of violence on children's development, the project particularly uses *Erikson's model of human development*. Erikson's approach suggests that development is characterised by specific crises to be resolved at various stages, and that to develop satisfactorily children need assistance to cope with these crises. Particular emphasis is placed on key "virtues" of trust, competence, identity and meaning. This approach is used in the Trust's workshops (see section 5.2 below).

Small infants quickly learn to *trust* their mothers to provide protection from hunger, cold and discomfort, and the growing child needs a sense of trust in parents (or other caretakers) to feel safe to explore the environment. Violence erodes trust; homelessness and separation, and the upheavals associated with violence militate against the protection and nurturance of children, and trust within families and within neighbourhoods is sometimes destroyed.

Children develop *competence* as they explore their environment through play, but violence against children promotes fear and insecurity, and children are inhibited from reaching out and exploring their surroundings. Education and other community activities which promote competence are disrupted.

Identity formation is the process by which young people understand themselves and their place in society. But breakdown in social norms during the period of political violence and actual involvement in violence interferes with this process, especially in adolescence. Family divisions exist because of differing political affiliations, and issues of ethnic identity can compound the problems in the formation of a strong sense of personal identity.

The term *meaning* refers to a way of viewing the world and interpreting events, and is informed by family experiences, wider social values, religious and political beliefs. Young people caught up in political violence may be confused and uncertain about their own belief systems and the meaning of the events in which they have become involved.

In the workshops, participants are encouraged to draw on their own experiences of child development and the way in which children known to them are affected by experiences of violence.

4.2 Indigenous Methods of Healing

Alongside Western approaches such as that of Erikson, emphasis is placed on indigenous methods of healing, which are explored in the workshops. The following is an example.

"*Ukukhipha igunga*" ("removing the instilled urge to kill") is a practice that rests on the notion that in order for a murderer to be rehabilitated completely, she/he is expected to undergo a certain cleansing process which is regarded as effective in removing the automatic urge to kill or engage in violence, an urge which lay behind such practices as "necklacing" (setting fire to a car tyre placed around someone's neck).

Religious beliefs also help people to make sense of their experiences. Spirituality is seen as important, whether beliefs in the spirits of the dead or Christian beliefs. Some of the independent African churches conduct large, community–based healing ceremonies.

4.3 Children's Games

Another important component of the training programme is the use of children's games as tools for diagnosing and treating violence–related trauma among children. The assumption underlying this approach is that the games played by children can highlight trauma–related concerns, and can be used to enable children to talk about experiences and express feelings about them.

One example is a popular game called *"Masiketlane"* which is played by a group of children in a circle. One of the players kneels at the centre, manipulates a small stone on the floor with the hands while simultaneously narrating a short story. While this takes place the other children clap their hands in a rhythmic form. Using the format of this game, children sometimes relate traumatic events from their own life experience.

Other singing and clapping games can be used, and *traditional proverbs, drawings and other "playful" approaches* are also utilised as means of communicating with children in ways which are culturally familiar. Issues such as anger and aggression can be addressed by using plays, poems, and singing as well as through discussion.

5. The Activities of the National Children and Violence Trust

The NCVT has three major components to its programme, training and capacity–building, trauma counselling and violence prevention. The activities carried out by the organisation include the creation of community–based networks, training workshops, direct provision of counselling, awareness creation and advocacy. Each of these will be considered in turn.

5.1 Community–based Networks

A number of local networks have been set up in different communities in order to make services of the project more accessible to communities in need. According to the Director of the Project, one of the most important achievements in 1994 was the establishment and development of community–based networks in four out of the nine provinces of South Africa, including some of those most affected by violence. These networks were formed by individuals from local communities who organised themselves into resource groups that respond to the psycho–social needs of traumatised children in their neighbourhoods.

The networks have their own offices, often shared with other organisations undertaking related work. Local co–ordinators are paid by NCVT and they work with large numbers of volunteers from the local community.

Sometimes referred to as networks of "front–line child care work-ers", they address trauma, facilitate reconciliation between children and adults, and bring together diverse people in the communities to respond to any problems concerning violence. Violence prevention – for example in schools – may be as important as assisting individu-als directly affected by violence.

Many of these networks were established in townships plagued by violence, which meant that outsiders were often reluctant to venture into them because of risk to their own safety. Mobilisation of these local networks served to lessen the dependence of these communities on outside assistance.

The *procedure for establishing a network* normally involves identifying local individuals who show some potential or interest in the activities of the project. In most cases such individuals are teachers, community workers, nurses, social workers and church workers. After initial contact with project staff, they are assisted by the Project Coordinator with the process of setting up the network. This involves *organising training workshops* in order to ensure that members of the network acquire the necessary skills for running the network activities. There are instances where the initial request for setting up a network comes from a community, often as a result of people's involvement in a training workshop.

In 1994, all the networks organised *strategic planning* exercises so as to define their own area of operation, identify prevalent forms of violence and make an annual plan. All these activities help the networks in focusing on the most pressing problems facing their particular communities and on the most appropriate strategies for responding to them. These exercises have helped to emphasise the importance of involving people across the community spectrum, all of whom need to be involved in the training workshops.

5.2 Training Workshops

Workshops are conducted nationally and locally with the aim of providing participants with an understanding of violence through analysing the social processes constituting such a problem, and to empower participants with the skills for working with child survivors of violence. The workshops are attended by a wide range of people, ranging from political activists, staff working for local authorities and members of NGOs to child care professionals such as nurses, social workers and teachers. Some workshops focus on more specialised topics such as rape. Generally, however, workshops focus on different forms of violence, their impact on children, on concepts of vulnerability and resilience, and intervention strategies. In order to maximise the understanding of the problem and the acquisition of skills, the following three steps are followed:

- the presentation of *theoretical perspectives* on the impact of violence on childhood development, the stress responses displayed by children and various intervention strategies (see section 4.1 above)
- *feedback and evaluation* by the participants, who are encouraged to *examine their own feelings* about violence against children. Case discussions and experiential group exercises examine the impact of violence on children and explore ways of assisting them
- detailed *action plans* are set out in order to encourage networking, ongoing support and skills training. It is vital to ensure a commitment and a mobilisation of resources

5.3 Counselling

The project provides counselling services to children and families affected by violence. They usually approach the Trust's offices, and specific days have been set aside for providing such services in all the community networks. In some cases the psychologists are contracted by the project to visit the local networks and clinics on specified days so as to provide counselling services to local people requiring them; in others, local psychologists, or specially trained lay counsellors would be used.

5.4 Violence Prevention

Violence prevention programmes usually consist of training and public awareness campaigns undertaken on a local level. Training is usually geared to those working with children and youth, and awareness programmes target the general public, especially young people and women. Schools, youth clubs and women's societies are particularly targeted. People are provided with information on how trauma and violence affect children, on alternative ways of resolving problems and so on.

5.5 Awareness Creation

The project utilises various strategies on a national and local level for the purposes of promoting awareness about violence and its effects on children. These strategies include campaigns, documentaries and newspaper articles.

Campaigns are usually organised together with groupings such as churches, para–statal and non–governmental organisations or other community–based groups. National campaigns are organised to create awareness about issues such as childhood trauma, child abuse and other acts of violence against children. During one of the campaigns conducted on Child Awareness Day, children carrying placards with messages on violence assembled at specific public points. Speeches were delivered by service providers so as to highlight the severity of the problem and to call for community participation in addressing it.

Documentaries on the project have been made. One film depicts childhood trauma in South Africa in the 1990s, while another addresses gender–specific forms of violence in collaboration with other organisations. Project staff have also participated in television programmes where topics on stress management and its impact on violence against children and child abuse were handled.

5.6 Advocacy

The NCVT involves various constitutuencies in advocating for policies, regulations and social programmes for those who are vulnerable and at risk. For example it works to develop violence curricula in schools, colleges and professional training institutions. More recently the Trust has been involved in the review of the Children Act.

The NCVT also conducts action research to inform the development of policies and social programmes to address societal violence and its impact on children, families and the community.

6. Analysis of Issues Arising from the Project

This section of the case study discusses some of the principal issues to emerge from an analysis of the operation of the National Children and Violence Trust.

6.1 Acknowledgement of Trauma as a Problem in African Communities

The lack of access to psychological services by disadvantaged communities in South Africa means that trauma could not be given serious attention. Those communities faced with problems of violence would simply have to accept them as a reality and attempt to devise some coping mechanisms. The work of the NCVT offers hope and a strong message that problems associated with violence–related trauma can still be addressed through appropriate psycho–social care. The resource base of the various communities has been enlarged by the participation of community members and practitioners such as social workers, nurses and teachers who develop skills in the workshops to encourage children who are victims of violence to use their experiences for the purpose of reconstructing their own futures.

The project has helped families to broaden their understanding of the challenges facing children during the various stages of development. The use of a participative educational approach in the workshops ensures that participants share their knowledge with the trainers, which is especially helpful in incorporating their knowledge of African cultural practices.

6.2 Empowerment of Communities

The NCVT relies on the participation of community members in its violence prevention programmes. Communities actively participate in the process of determining the needs of and priorities for their local networks. As communities participate in community education programmes and in workshops on the problem of violence in society, they gain insight on both the extent and possible strategies for addressing the problem.

Participation is empowering to community members as it enables them to become the *main actors* in their local programmes as opposed to outsiders such as professionals from the national office determining their agenda. Such participation is also crucial for the *sustainability* of the programmes and for the *affirmation of communities as sources of knowledge*. There is less dependence on outsiders as communities play a primary role in the planning and implementation of their own programmes. The role played by the Trust's national office is secondary as it only facilitates the process through providing guidance and knowledge where necessary.

Community members have a better understanding of their local dynamics and are thus in a better position to make accurate assessments of need. They are able to become more self–reliant, while the culture of participation becomes integrated into the community's lifestyle, resulting in stronger tendencies towards self–determination. Communities gain a sense of ownership both of the problem of violence, and of the means of responding in ways which suit local circumstances.

6.3 Community–based Networks as Catalysts of a New Culture

During the apartheid era, the access of black communities to government resources was restricted by discriminatory laws, and this militated against the capacity of families to meet the needs of their children. In turn this served to increase the demand for institutional care, but most residential homes were overcrowded, understaffed and generally unsatisfactory. Community networks became catalysts of a new culture that rests on the notion that the family and community–based care is the best option for families.

6.4 Recognition of Indigenous Methods of Healing

There are deeply ingrained African beliefs and practices associated with issues of violence and healing. The colonisers consciously undermined many aspects of African culture, labelling it "primitive" and emphasising Western values and practices. In addition, many Christian churches discouraged the use of indigenous methods of healing. Negative attitudes to African culture have also served to discourage the exchange of information between modern and African approaches to health care. Nevertheless, many Africans secretly adhere to these beliefs and practices.

The problems of violence–related trauma have pervaded all aspects of South African society. Given the limited psychological services in the disadvantaged communities, it is imperative that every possible resource be mobilised and that indigenous healing is recognised as a reality. Furthermore, the NCVT realised that traditional healers should be provided with education on modern approaches to therapy.

The strategy of the Trust is to refrain from passing judgement about indigenous methods of healing, but rather to *encourage traditional healers* and their communities to open up to new approaches to psychological healing. Traditional healers are encouraged to attend the workshops so as to exchange information and ideas for the purposes of fostering collaboration. When people feel respected and understood they are more likely to respond positively to new ideas. By addressing these cultural beliefs, the project becomes more acceptable to traditional communities, and people are more likely to utilise services that are sensitive to their cultural orientation.

6.5 Linkages between Political and Domestic Violence

The previous National Party government did not foster the values of tolerance for racial, ethnic and political differences. Tendencies towards intolerance and hostility were internalised by members of South African society as viable means of conflict resolution, culminating in extreme cases of political violence.

One of the consequences of political violence has been the destabilisation of many aspects of society such as the economic, housing and educational sectors. Political violence has crippled the economy, resulting in a high unemployment rate and an increase in poverty. It has increased the number of homeless people as homes were destroyed during the factional fighting and people fled areas plagued by violence. This has resulted in the increased number of informal settlements in which conditions of overcrowding and lack of resources militate against the preservation of family life and the moral fabric of society. Indeed they foster the breakdown of family values of respect and protection of the vulnerable, which is evident in the *different forms of domestic violence* such as spouse abuse and violence against children. With the destabilisation of communities, the family's capacity to nurture and protect its children is reduced.

On the other hand, domestic violence can also be regarded as one of the causal factors underlying political violence. It may be that children who grow up in households where domestic violence is rife are more likely to be perpetrators of political violence since they may have internalised the values of intolerance and hostility.

The NCVT has been dealing with many cases where domestic violence seems to be closely related to political violence. While the initial purpose of the project was to address the problems of political violence, services delivered had to be broadened so as to address other related forms of violence such as domestic, sexual and school–based violence.

6.6 Cost–effectiveness

The high demand for the services of the Children and Violence Trust in the communities of South Africa is evident in the large number of individuals seeking the services of the Trust and participation in the workshops which are conducted on a regular basis. It is clear that given the project's limited resources, it would be impossible for it to meet the demand when operating solely from its national offices. The strategy of establishing community–based networks in the various communities seems to be appropriate for efficient service–delivery. The services of the project become more accessible to communities since they are saved from the long trips which they otherwise would undertake to and from the national office. Local volunteers and co–ordinators are able to plan and render services with very modest budgets.

The project also relies on the services of other professionals on a part–time or temporary basis. For example, a number of networks rely on counsellors who are not employed on a full time basis. While this reduces the costs of the project, it still has its disadvantages as it militates against the stability and continuity which is really required by counselling services.

6.7 The Need to Support Front Line Care Workers

It is the experience of the Trust that many of the people involved in the workshops and in the neighbourhood networks have had difficult experiences of violence themselves. Indeed involvement in the project's activities may actually attract people with such experiences. Because of this, not only do the workshops encourage the participants to examine and analyse their own experience, but the need for support systems is also acknowledged. Enrichment programmes, support networks and peer–support systems are an important part of the Trust's work.

6.8 Adaptability

South Africa is now undergoing rapid changes as a result of political transformation. For any project to be effective it has to adapt to social change. A project that deals with children and youth has to constantly review its strategies in order to maintain its relevance to the target group. The strategic planning exercises undertaken by each network ensure that needs are re–assessed, that activities undertaken are appropriate to the particular social context, and that these activities are critically reviewed and evaluated. While information is shared between all the networks, care is taken that uniformity is not emphasised to the extent of undermining the *diversity of needs and resources* in different communities.

7. Conclusions

The National Children and Violence Trust has helped in bringing the problem of violence against children to the attention of communities, professionals and policy–makers. Project staff have been part of a well–known interest group acting as a watchdog for the interests and rights of children and families affected by violence. For example, they have been making an input into the unfolding of the government's Reconstruction and Development Programme, and have been involved in the process of revising the Children's Act.

While this case study was being conducted, the Director of the NCVT left the University to take up the position of a Director of Mental Health Services in the national government offices. The staff members of the NCVT admit that the new democratic government needs people of the calibre of Mrs. Mkhize. However, they also realise the challenge posed by such a major change within the organisation which has made her Honorary Director with reduced availability to the project. But it is also realised that her appointment further validates the relevance of the mental health care approach developed within the CVT.

The Trust is well positioned to strengthen the already existing relationships with other organisations concerned with violence in society. The government's strategy of service–delivery emphasises co–operation with NGOs through a primary health care approach, which bodes well for the future role of the Children and Violence Trust in the new South Africa.

Timely Social Work Intervention in Refugee Emergencies: the Work of the Standby Team

by David Tolfree

1. Introduction

Until comparatively recently, when refugee emergencies occurred, the main emphasis for the United Nations High Commission for Refugees (UNHCR) and other relief agencies in the early weeks and months was to provide essential, life–sustaining measures such as shelter, food, water and sanitation, health care and legal protection. Work to identify particularly vulnerable groups of refugees (single parent families, unaccompanied children, people with disabilities, severely traumatised children and adults, and so on) and the development of social services to meet their needs was seen as less essential and less urgent – perhaps even a "luxury" which could wait until other, more pressing needs had been met.

Increasingly, however, this approach has been questioned by organisations such as Rädda Barnen, and though it is obvious that life–sustaining measures should be accorded the highest priority, this does not detract from the urgency of work to identify vulnerable refugees and to plan ways of ensuring that their needs are met. Two factors particularly emphasised the importance and urgency of work within what has become known as community services in refugee emergencies: first, there has been a growing awareness of the non-material needs of particularly vulnerable refugees, especially children and women. Large numbers of unaccompanied children, the problems faced by single-parent families, and the high incidence of refugees who have been exposed to violence and conflict have been notable features of many refugee emergencies. Second, there has been a growing recognition that it is vital to encourage and enable refugees, at an early stage, to take responsibility both for the assessment of social needs and for the planning and implementation of appropriate ways of meeting those needs. Failure to do so has demonstrably resulted in a growing sense of dependence, and an increasing reliance on "welfare services" provided by external agencies rather than a sense of "ownership" both of the problems and of the means of tackling them.

In the early years of the present decade, there was, within UNHCR, a growing recognition of the need to "mainstream" responses to the needs of refugee children and women, and to promote the Refugee Children Guidelines[6]. UNHCR also acknowledged the need to improve its general response to emergency situations – a need highlighted by their experience with Kurdish refugees and the situation arising from the Gulf War. These concerns resulted in the decision to establish Emergency Reponse Teams under the leadership of Emergency Preparedness and Response Officers (EPROs), and which included various categories of staff seconded to UNHCR by other NGOs. While these developments were taking place, Rädda Barnen were seeking ways both of becoming more involved in emergency situations (but without, however, engaging in general relief work) and in drawing on its extensive experience of psycho–social work with refugee children.

With these factors in mind, Rädda Barnen decided to establish a standby capacity of 20 experienced social workers who would be available at short notice for deployment in emergency situations. Then in May 1993, a formal agreement was made with UNHCR for Rädda Barnen to provide, at 72 hours notice, a minimum of six qualified and experienced staff to join their Emergency Response

Teams as Community Services Officers (CSOs), to provide early needs assessments, and to begin to facilitate the setting up of refugee structures and encourage their active involvement in responding to the needs of particularly vulnerable refugees, especially those of children and women. The CSOs worked as members of the UNHCR Emergency Teams, accountable to the EPRO but funded by Rädda Barnen.

The first two deployments of members of the Standby Team occurred very quickly after the initial training, and a number of other deployments occurred during 1993. Early in 1994, the tragic events in Rwanda led to the huge exodus of refugees into neighbouring countries, and a total of four deployments were arranged. One of these involved a group of refugee camps in the Karagwe District of Tanzania. This deployment is the focus of this case study.

2. Methodology

For the purpose of compiling this case study, it was felt important not just to examine the work of the CSO, but also to consider the "legacy" of the deployment by examining the subsequent development of community services in the refugee camps. With this in mind it was decided to visit this group of camps with the person who had undertaken the CSO mission about three months earlier. This visit therefore combined an examination of the work she had already undertaken, with an exploration of subsequent work, primarily by Save the Children Fund UK (SCF(UK)) who had taken the lead role in providing and coordinating community services.

The principal methodologies employed were:
- *semi–structured interviews* with key informants, particularly with the former CSO, other Rädda Barnen staff, personnel in UNHCR, SCF (UK) and other NGOs
- *field visits and observation*, including participant observation in a training seminar and informal discussions with refugees
- *a review of documentation* provided by Rädda Barnen, UNHCR and Save the Children (UK).

- *a draft copy of the case study was shared with key Rädda Barnen staff* and amendments made in the light of their comments

3. The Community Services Officer Deployment and Subsequent Developments

Following the tragic wave of massacres in Rwanda in the period of April–August 1994, more than 2 million refugees fled to neighbouring countries. About 110,000 sought refuge in Karagwe, a remote district in the northwest of Tanzania: about 4 times that number settled in the Ngara District further south.

In Karagwe, the refugees were settled in five camps in three main areas which were some considerable distances apart, in inaccessible areas making for extreme transportation difficulties. Many of the refugees arrived in a poor physical condition, having travelled on foot for many days before crossing the Kagera River or Lake Rushwa. Most came from rural parts of Rwanda, the vast majority were Hutus and the general level of education was low.

The main components of the CSO's *terms of reference* were
- to assess immediate needs within the refugee communities and identify ways and means to meet them
- to identify and support existing community structures within the refugee communities
- to establish a programme for the identification of vulnerable refugees – notably unaccompanied children – and to begin the development of a family tracing and reunification programme and other programmes to meet the needs of vulnerable groups
- to identify NGOs which might play a part in the development of community services and to provide training and capacity building where necessary

The CSO faced many constraints in pursuing these objectives. Apart from the practical difficulties presented by a large refugee influx scattered in remote areas, there was a lack of continuity within the Emergency Response Team. It was clear from the beginning of this deployment that while, on the one hand, there were large numbers of vulnerable refugees, notably unaccompanied children, on the other there was a *lack of NGOs* interested and experienced in this area of work. An additional problem was that of recruiting, from among the refugees, people with the capacity to be trained in social work skills.

However, one NGO with experience of working in Rwanda (but not experienced in community services) was keen to cooperate and undertook a survey of vulnerable groups (with particular emphasis on unaccompanied children) in two of the camps, under the supervision of the CSO. Secondary school students were trained and deployed to conduct the survey. In two camps (located close together), another NGO agreed to assist in the process of identifying and documenting unaccompanied children. This NGO, though having two social workers, had little experience of community services and, as will be discussed below, adopted some singularly inappropriate policies in these camps. In the fifth camp, a health–oriented NGO caried out a survey aimed at identifying unaccompanied children.

The first survey revealed an *exceptionally large number of unaccompanied children* – about 16% of all children, about half of whom were living with unrelated families. It also revealed a large number of single parent families, including an unusually large number of male–headed families, and the heavy workload of women – especially single women – was recognised. Another NGO conducted a survey of elderly and disabled refugees in one of the camps, revealing a high number of elderly refugees but a relatively small number of people with severe disabilities.

It was clear from the information collected that the major focus for community services would be arranging and supporting care arrangements for unaccompanied children, initiating, with the International Committee of the Red Cross (ICRC) a family tracing and reunification programme, and developing a programme of activities for young people as a means of facilitating their recovery from traumatic experiences.

Elections were held for community leaders: one man and one woman from each zone were elected to form zone committees. In addition, steps were taken to set up *community services sub–committees* which, it was envisaged, would help in a variety of tasks, including the surveys of vulnerable refugees, and the identification of potential carers for unaccompanied children. Attempts were made to *recruit "social supporters"* from within the refugee communities, and to provide training and supervision to enable them to carry out a variety of tasks in community services such as interviewing unaccompanied children and other vulnerable groups, interviewing potential carers and arranging and supporting placements.

A major issue was *identifying additional NGOs* to assist in the very substantial task of working in the community services sector and to coordinate what might become a very fragmented pattern of support. After the end of the CSO's deployment, and following an unfortunate delay caused by inter–agency misunderstandings, SCF(UK) began a major programme in the District and deployed a team of workers to carry on her work, and by the time of the field visit (some three months after the end of the CSO's deployment) they had established a programme which was building effectively on her assessment and planning. SCF (UK), along with various other NGOs were deploying, on a large scale, "community supporters", who were recruited from among the refugees, and great progress had been made in identifying and documenting unaccompanied children, arranging and supporting foster placements, and developing cultural and recreational activities.

Although Rädda Barnen recognises the *central importance of developing educational facilities* early on in a refugee emergency, the wide range of demands on the CSO and the priority which was given, appropriately, to the needs of unaccompanied children conspired to create a situation in which little could be done to begin the task of promoting education in the camps in the emergency phase. However, the facilitation of leadership structures was a significant step in this direction, and the strategy of encouraging refugee initiatives provided the background against which some informal

147

"schools" started spontaneously, often involving groups of children, sitting under trees and engaging in a variety of activities under the leadership of teachers, priests or other committed individuals. A number of NGOs were providing programmes of recreational activities, including sports, music and dancing, and a variety of activities were targeted towards refugee women.

On a regional level, UNHCR, Unicef and UNESCO worked together with the Government of Tanzania and a major donor to plan educational provision in the camps, devise appropriate curricula, develop and supply teachers' kits and ensure the provision of appropriate technical support. The camps in Karagwe were the last to benefit from this initiative, but nevertheless at the time of the field visit, a great deal of activity was in evidence, teachers were beginning their training, and school buildings were being erected.

4. Discussion and Analysis

In this section there will be a discussion of some of the principal issues to emerge from this experience of the deployment of a CSO early in what was a large refugee influx which presented an unusually large concentration of social problems.

4.1 The Importance of Early Community Services Intervention

The Standby Team was initiated in the belief that, whilst life–sustaining needs should obviously be given the first priority in a refugee emergency, it is also of vital importance that other needs and problems are addressed at an early stage. The experience in Karagwe offered ample confirmation of this, with three points standing out as having central importance.

First, the deployment proved effective in *enabling refugees themselves to take responsibility for the many social problems* in the camps, and not slide into a dependent attitude that they are "someone else's responsibility". Although it is intrinsically difficult to measure refugee participation, it seemed that the CSO successfully worked with refugees themselves, and with various colleagues in UNHCR and other NGOs to emphasise the vital importance of external intervention being seen as supplementing and reinforcing, but not replacing, the endeavours of the refugees themselves to identify, assess and find solutions to the many problems they were facing. The need to facilitate the participation of refugee women, and to support the women's own initiatives to organise themselves was seen to be especially important[7].

By facilitating leadership structures, including community services sub–committees, within the refugee community, the responsibilities and *potential for responsiveness of the refugees were enhanced*, and a sense of partnership with external agencies was initiated. This is in stark contrast with other refugee situations in which the refugees perceive themselves to be passive recipients of social services rather than active participants in the tasks of identifying problems and developing solutions.

Second, the deployment was significant in helping to *avoid inappropriate responses* to social problems. In one particular camp a great deal of energy was expended by one NGO in promoting institutional responses to the needs of unaccompanied children, and, in the process, generated a great deal of media interest which served to generate funds. The CSO acted quickly to reinforce UNHCR's policy of community–based care, to work with this particular NGO to encourage and facilitate the closure of the institution and the development of more appropriate alternatives. It seems highly likely that had the CSO not been involved at this early stage, there would have been a proliferation of institutions which would quickly stimulate demand which would be impossible to meet. Apart from the inappropriateness of institutional care, such developments severely detract from the philosophy of facilitating refugee responsibility.

Another example of the importance of avoiding inappropriate solutions was the work done to regularise the placement of children in foster care. A balance was struck between, on the one hand not discouraging individual refugees from taking responsibility for the care of unaccompanied children, while on the other hand introducing some regulating mechanisms which served to reinforce community responsibility for these children and provide some safeguards to protect children from the possibility of abuse.

Finally, the deployment of the CSO was effective in *sensitising* refugees themselves and both UNHCR and NGOs to the *needs and problems of vulnerable groups*. An enhanced awareness of the situation of unaccompanied children, of single parent families and of particularly vulnerable women, for example, appeared to have an impact throughout the camps in enabling refugees to be seen as "whole people" and to avoid the narrow focus on physical needs which has characterised many refugee programmes in the past.

4.2 The Importance of Early Work with Unaccompanied Children

In many past refugee emergencies, work with unaccompanied children has not been given high priority. In Malawi, for example, it was almost four years after the beginning of the Mozambican refugee emergency that the first systematic work was started to interview and document unaccompanied children and take steps to trace their families[8]. This is clearly an area in which delay is damaging. Apart from the extreme anxiety and distress faced by separated children and their families, memories of the circumstances of separation from their families will fade and the practical difficulties in tracing families will be greater. Moreover, children placed with other families will develop new attachments, and the likely disruption to those attachments caused by family reunification will increase as time passes. These points serve to emphasise the importance of family tracing programmes being established as early as possible in the emergency phase[9].

It is also vitally important that children who have become separated from their families are placed within families which can meet their needs adequately. Within the Rwandese refugee community, large numbers of unaccompanied children were *absorbed spontaneously into families*, many of them unrelated. Fortunately in Rwandese culture there is a tradition of caring for parentless children in families even where there is no blood tie, but it was also clear that the potential for abuse does exist. It is therefore vital that the initiatives of families are supplemented by those of refugee leaders, UNHCR and NGOs to *facilitate appropriate placements* and to *provide some monitoring and support* to fostered children and their caregivers. At the time of the follow–up visit to Karagwe, this work was progressing extremely well, though there was some evidence that the risks involved in fostering were not being adequately weighed and that, despite the scale of the problem, more needed to be done to ensure the safety and well–being of children in foster care. On the other hand, support and monitoring were being seen as a community responsibility, and steps had been taken to avoid an over–professionalised response.

On a regional basis, the ICRC had been given the mandate for the regional coordination and implementation of the family tracing and reunification programme. At the time of the follow–up visit, this was not working satisfactorily. Instead of integrating family tracing and reunification efforts with the task of supporting unaccompanied children within the community, interviewing and documentation was seen as a discrete task, undertaken by ICRC on the basis of the minimum necessary information being recorded. Full life histories were not being taken, and this vital information, which requires sensitive and painstaking work to elicit, was in danger of being lost as memories fade. The lack of a team ethos between ICRC and the other agencies involved with children was a particularly significant weakness.

In refugee situations, *decision making must be based on the totality of the child's experience* – past, present and future, and be based on a *clear judgement of his/her best interests*. In Karagwe this was not happening consistently because services had become fragmented.

4.3 Capacity–building within NGOs

A significant aspect of the role of the CSO is that of capacity–building with NGOs who are in a position to assist with the refugee emergency. Karagwe was not well–endowed with NGOs, though there were a number of locally based organisations which had an interest – though little experience – in community services. An important part of the CSO's role was therefore to offer *professional advice and guidance, training and coordination of NGOs*, especially those who were able to make a contribution to community services. As already indicated, the prevention of inappropriate responses as well as the positive promotion of programmes and approaches were important aspects of her role.

Given the constraints of the large number of refugees located in camps some considerable distance from each other, and also the large concentration of unaccompanied children and other vulnerable groups, the three–months duration of the deployment did not provide sufficient time for this important work of capacity–building, and it was interesting to see that SCF (UK) had taken up this role and were promoting it strongly. The role of the CSO would have been greatly enhanced by supplementing it with the *deployment of an experienced community services trainer* at the vital, early stage in the emergency when the groundwork was being laid for the development of community services. This would probably have been significant in influencing both the policies and practices of NGOs and might have helped to avoid the unfortunate institution–building approach of one NGO.

4.4 Facilitating Refugees' Recovery from Traumatic Experiences

One of the most striking characteristics of the Rwandese refugees was their *high level of exposure to experiences of violence* as well as displacement which would be expected to have a traumatising effect. A significant finding of a survey of children was that 63% of separated children had witnessed killings and that almost a third had seen their own parents being killed[10].

The follow–up visit to Karagwe suggested that, on the one hand there was some concern amongst UNHCR and NGO staff about the effects of such experiences both on current functioning and on future mental health. On the other hand, mental health understandings were not in evidence in the mainstream thinking and planning of agencies, and where there was an awareness of such issues, there was a general feeling of inadequacy in not being able to respond. Following the lead offered by the CSO deployed in the emergency phase, NGOs such as SCF (UK) were focussing their efforts on providing and supporting appropriate care arrangements for unaccompanied children, emphasising the importance and urgency of family tracing, and supporting the provision of meaningful activities for children, whether in the form of cultural and recreational activities, sports or informal schools.

These were undoubtedly appropriate priorities, but left open the question of how the most seriously affected children (and adults) could be assisted. Moreover, it seemed that the issue of the psychological affects of violence and displacement were being conceptualised as *individual problems rather than as the concern of the whole community*. Those agencies who were attempting to respond to individuals seeking help with psychological problems had access only to Western approaches which emphasised counselling skills. But in Rwandese society such approaches are not only unfamiliar but culturally inappropriate, given that people were accustomed to talking intimately only with very close family and friends.

What seemed to be needed was an approach which defined the problem as shared by the community, one which could be openly recognised and talked about, and which sought to use approaches which are both culturally sensitive and perceived by the refugees as helpful. A serious lack was the limited opportunities for religious practice and the comfort which that may bring for many people. Furthermore, one of the effects of experiences of violence seemed to be people's withdrawal from social and religious contacts, creating a vicious circle.

Work was, however, being done to incorporate into the curriculum for teacher training, knowledge about the psychological effects of war and techniques for assisting troubled children. This seemed likely to be an important move to reach out to the more troubled children.

The majority of the refugees were Christian. There seemed to be a vital role for the churches in providing comfort and healing to people affected by their experiences of war and violence. However, in some camps there was a lack of priests, and more generally among agencies there was a lack of recognition of the need to see the church as having an important role in this difficult area. An added problem was that people were aware that some priests had been involved in atrocities in Rwanda.

4.5 The Importance of the early Re-establishment of Education

Responsibility for undertaking the initial work of planning educational facilities for refugee children is seen as part of the role of the CSO within the Emergency Team. In Karagwe, however, the size and geographical spread of the refugee population, coupled with the need to prioritise the needs of unaccompanied children, created a situation where it was difficult for the CSO to be very involved in this area, though on a regional level, formal education was being planned from a very early stage.

Some activities, including *informal schooling* for groups of children sitting in the shade of trees, were initiated by the refugees themselves. However, few appropriate material resources were available during the early period of the emergency, and little was done to further encourage and stimulate this kind of development.

The real significance of early initiatives to begin educational activities lies in the urgency to create for children, especially those who have been distressed by their experiences, *a structure to their daily lives, a sense of purpose, and the rewards of achievement* and the self–esteem that result from it. Participation in educational activities also provides young people not only with a sense of future, but an opportunity to invest in that future. This is vital in helping to avoid the passive dependence and sense of hopelessness and despair that can so easily characterise refugee camps. It is with these objectives in mind that educational activity is so valuable, long before the stage where it is possible to implement more formal education, with trained teachers, an agreed curriculum and school buildings. Despite the many and potentially competing priorities facing the CSO in an emergency situation, it is important that time, and modest material resources, are found to facilitate and support the endeavours of refugees themselves in beginning to meet children's urgent need for educational opportunities.

4.6 Developing Understanding of the Refugees' Culture and Community Resources

An important aspect of the work of the CSO within the Emergency Team is to build up a *good understanding not just of the refugees' problems and needs, but also their resources* – their culture and traditions, their approaches and skills in handling problems and coping with difficulties, their human resources and patterns of comunity leadership and their own perception of their needs and priorities. In seeking to help facilitate the setting–up of refugee structures, it is vital for the CSO to understand the leadership patterns typical in the country of origin, the role of women within the community and so on. It seems that this is a deceptively difficult task, especially for a white expatriate worker with no prior knowledge of the culture. An added problem is that no system exists for accessing socio–cultural information prior to the CSO's deployment.

CSOs have different approaches to building up these understandings: refugees themselves are the most obvious source of information, with interpreters hired from within the refugee community playing a particularly important role. The follow–up visit to Karagwe gave the impression that programmes were being developed on the basis of incomplete understandings of the culture of the refugees. Even for agencies that wanted to address the psychological health of refugees distressed by their experiences of violence and flight, there seemed to be very limited understanding of how Rwandese people deal with death, loss and personal stress. Finding ways of rapidly accessing existing anthropological information, and developing tools for eliciting appropriate socio–cultural information from the refugees themselves are two challenges for the future.

One of the unusual characteristics of some of the camps in Ngara was that refugees were settled within their original community groupings[11], and when it was necessary to move some of the refugees away from the most crowded camp in Karagwe, it was decided to pursue a similar model. This presented enormous advantages in recreating some of the original structures and support networks within the community. It also promoted a sense of community solidarity and responsibility, enhancing the possibility of fostering children with members of the community who would be able to continue to provide sustainable care in the event of repatriation.

5. Conclusions

The now–routine deployment of a CSO within UNHCR's Emergency Team is possibly one of the most significant developments in promoting an understanding of, and prompt responses to, the problems, needs and resources of particularly vulnerable refugees, especially children. The broad scope of the role, coupled with the huge scale and scattered population of refugees in Karagwe, made for an exceptionally demanding assignment.

Yet despite the many constraints faced by the CSO, her work was highly successful in *highlighting the needs of the most vulnerable* amongst the refugees, most notably the exceptionally large population of unaccompanied children, many of whom had had the most appalling experiences of violence as well as the hardships of flight and the many constraints of refugee camp life. The follow–up visit to Karagwe demonstrated that her work had been effectively followed up by NGOs who took over where she left off. Particularly significant was her work in *facilitating the setting–up of community structures*, in assessing and responding to the immediate problems and *care needs of unaccompanied children*, and in the difficult tasks of *developing the capacity of local NGOs* to be able to respond effectively in an area of work in which they lacked experience.

The deployment of a CSO in an emergency can be seen as a very cost–effective measure. A period as short as three months does seem to be sufficient for a highly experienced social worker to undertake the initial work on assessing needs, facilitating the setting–up of community structures, involving refugees in planning and beginning to implement programmes in the priority areas identified.

The community–mobilisation approach, in contrast with the traditional individually oriented social work approach, means that large numbers of refugees can be reached without the necessity of deploying large numbers of specialist staff to undertake direct work with children and families. The approach has the great advantage of *capacitating both refugees and local NGOs* in such a way that their own resources are strengthened by new knowledge, skills and experience. The active engagement with refugees is highly significant in helping to avoid the passive dependence which can have extremely serious and long–term consequences – and while refugee empowerment and mobilisation are, by their nature, difficult to measure, the effects were to be seen in Karagwe.

One of the major challenges to emerge from this experience is to find ways in which the role of a single CSO in such a large–scale emergency can be supplemented in order to give greater attention to *early educational developments* and to ensure that the exceptionally large numbers of unaccompanied children benefit from *comprehensive and integrated programmes of care, support and family tracing*. Another challenge posed by the Rwandan refugee emergency is for Rädda Barnen and UNHCR to find ways of responding more comprehensively to the *mental health needs of refugee children in a way that is consistent with the community–based approach.*

There can be little doubt that Rädda Barnen's Standby Team has been highly effective in raising the profile of children and their particular needs in refugee situations. It has also given added impetus to the implementation of the Guidelines on Refugee Children[12]. The Standby Agreement with UNHCR has helped to restore the credibility of social work in refugee emergencies by promoting a model that is effective, cost–effective, and, most significantly, encourages refugee initiative rather than passive dependency.

Building on Traditional Strengths: the Unaccompanied Refugee Children from South Sudan

by Hirut Tefferi

1. Background and Context

Sudan is the largest country in Africa with an area of 2.5 million square kilometres and a population of approximately 25 million people. It is a country with huge potential but is at present one of Africa's poorest. This has mainly been the result of many years of civil war which has been going on since 1966, with a relative period of peace from 1972 – 1983. The war is between the Islamic Government in the north and the Sudan People's Liberation Movement (SPLM) in the mainly Christian south, and has resulted in displacement of a large number of southern Sudanese into the neighbouring countries. The United Nations High Commission for Refugees (UNHCR) estimates about 300,000 Sudanese refugees in Uganda, 45,000 in Kenya and 50,000 in Ethiopia. There are more Sudanese refugees in the Central African Republic, Zaire and Egypt.

In 1987 there was a particularly large influx of Sudanese refugees into the Gambella region of Ethiopia. Among them was a large group (approximately 14,000) of unaccompanied children, mainly boys, mostly aged between 9 and 14 years, who settled in Pignudo camp, after an extended period of travelling in the face of severe hardships and dangers. While it is not entirely clear why such a group of unaccompanied children sought refuge, the SPLM were certainly actively involved in the exodus and in organising care arrangements for the children in Pignudo. In 1991, following the change of government in Ethiopia and a shift in political alliances, these young people migrated through southern Sudan, in the face of further traumatic and horrifying difficulties, finally arriving in Kakuma, Kenya where they are presently camped.

In Kakuma, UNHCR oversees the protection of all refugees and monitors the activities in the camp. The Lutheran World Federation (LWF) is in charge of the overall running of the camp, sanitation, and social services. The International Rescue Committee (IRC) conducts primary health care, and the Don Bosco organisation implements vocational training in carpentry and masonry. Rädda Barnen implements psycho–social and, from 1994, educational programmes.

This case study attempts to give an overview of Rädda Barnen's experience of working with this large group of unaccompanied children in the Pignudo camp in Ethiopia and later on in the Kakuma refugee camp in Kenya. It covers nearly 8 years of work with only a few months of Rädda Barnen's absence from the project sites. Throughout this period, Rädda Barnen staff were instrumental in developing strategies for working with war affected children, initiating and witnessing changes, in the ever–changing socio–political context in the horn of Africa.

2. Methodology

The main methodologies used in the compiling of this case study are the following:

- the *author's own experience* and that of other staff working in the field over a period of approximately eight years
- *statistical information* drawn from UNHCR reports and Rädda Barnen's periodical monitoring and evaluation reports.
- *review of documentation* including –

- internal project assessments
- various UNHCR and Rädda Barnen monitoring and
  evaluation reports
- a study based on a large collection of personal histories of
  unaccompanied children
• *direct participation* in field workshops and *observation of specific
  field activities* designed to supplement the information gathered
  by the methodologies outlined above
• notes on observations were *shared with refugees* in Kakuma, and
  the findings and interpretations were also shared and discussed
  in a *workshop* held with a wide range of interested people in
  Nairobi

3. Description of the Project

Rädda Barnen's intervention in the Pignudo refugee camp in
Ethiopia started in 1988, in cooperation with the UNHCR. At the
time, Rädda Barnen was the only international NGO which was
allowed, by the Ethiopian government, to have access to the refugee
camp. According to a UNHCR report in Pignudo there were over
13,000 unaccompanied children between 6 and 15 years of age by
the beginning of 1988. Rädda Barnen assisted with relief goods,
while establishing appropriate psycho–social interventions;
responding to the special needs of the large number of
unaccompanied children in the camp was a particular priority.

The Pignudo project for unaccompanied refugee children started
off with the documentation of the history of individual children,
primary education, preventive and curative mental health programmes, placement of new arrivals and organising care programmes in
group and foster care.

Based on this experience, Rädda Barnen later initiated psycho–
social activities in Kakuma and southern Sudan to provide
assistance to war traumatised children in a social and cultural
context. A highly significant feature in the background of these
children was the fact of having had *multiple experiences of violence,
separation and the physical and emotional demands* of the long walk to

exile in Ethiopia, and subsequently in the long and *again traumatising journey* through Sudan into Kenya. The programme was designed to take care of psychological development of individuals in relation to their social and cultural environment. It provided opportunity and built capacity for the social integration of the refugee population during and after the refugee emergency.

The programme in Kakuma has the following components:

3.1 Group Care

This is a care programme catering for unaccompanied children who are over 14 years of age. There are 19 groups each consisting of up to 250 children organised into villages of up to 50 children and subsequently divided into sub–groups of 3 – 5, living together in one tukul (hut) under the supervision of care–takers employed from among the refugees. Unaccompanied children grouped themselves voluntarily, based on kinship and other social relationships, while in Pignudo the grouping was done on the basis of age and level of education.

The arrangement is *adapted from a traditional practice* of the Sudanese in which groups of boys live for certain periods in cattle camps, often a long distance from their homes. The practice was first introduced in Pignudo refugee camp by the refugees themselves and has since been modified to adequately address the needs of the children. These traditional practices seem to serve to protect children from the worst effects of separation from their parents, and the practice of peer–group living in the cattle camps served to prepare children for the form of group–care in the refugee camps.

3.2 Foster Care

Prior to the implementation of this programme by Rädda Barnen, social workers opened discussions with the refugee community on the subject of foster care. Some members of the community supported the idea of having children fostered with families in the camp based on their traditional practice of caring for unattached children within families. Others thought that since the children would need to pursue education they can only do so effectively if the children were organised to live in groups of their own as in boarding schools.

Finally it was decided by the community to start foster care as a *pilot project* with volunteer families, but that the children themselves should take the *initiative in choosing their foster families*. Foster families would then provide the necessary support to the fostered children in a home environment. Information was passed to minors who formed themselves into groups of 3 or 4 and approached the social workers with a name of the family they wished to live with. The social workers met with such families and where their agreement was obtained, they supported the children to build a hut next to that of the selected family.

Foster care is an arrangement designed to cater for the needs of children under 14 years of age. In addition, those who have been known to be especially vulnerable owing to a history of mental disturbance, chronic physical illness such as TB, or the occurrence of a recent traumatic experience are placed with families for appropriate support.

The concept of fostering in the camp is a *diverse one*: some small groups of older boys live in a separate hut, receiving only minimum support from the foster parents, while for other, especially younger children, there is a greater sense of membership of, and integration with the foster family.

Rädda Barnen supports this arrangement through the periodic provision of material needs such as soap, sugar, and other supplies. The material input provided by Rädda Barnen is intended to reach children living with regular families as well, so as to avoid creating a situation where unaccompanied children are perceived as a materially priveleged group. Fostering is also supported and monitored by visiting social workers recruited from among the refugees.

Although the fostering has a positive impact on the fostered children, it may have *added to the burden of girls and women*. Although major decisions in this culture tend to be taken by men, it is the women and girls who carry the main responsibility for child care. The effect of the foster care programme on the status of women in the family, and on the school attendance of the girls in the fostering families, needs further study.

3.3 Preventive Mental Health Care

This is a programme designed to address the possible effects of trauma in children through the use of preventive interventions. It aims to reduce the impact of war among the children through encouraging the expression of feelings in culturally acceptable ways and encourages the involvement of supportive institutions to promote better mental health conditions for the children.

In Pignudo, it was found necessary to develop a *mental health unit*, which provided intensive psychological support to children so severely affected by their experiences that they could not cope adequately with "home" and school life. Problems such as aggression, withdrawal and depression were the most common symptoms. However, the numbers of children needing this kind of intensive support were small (less than 1%), and this figure has now declined to almost nil, rendering this kind of residential facility unnecessary. The principal approach to mental health has been preventive rather than curative.

Many young people are involved in *religious activities*. Rädda Barnen's initiatives in this area are supplemented very positively by the religious leaders and through the guiding roles of the *leaders and traditional healers* in the camp. Many refugees express their feelings of distress and insecurity during church services.

The programme assists children to adjust positively to their current situation. Emphasis is placed on identifying and providing assistance to vulnerable children through *community based group activities* such as child–to–child programmes, story–telling, poetry, dream–groups, art and craft, scouting, football, etc.. Through such programmes children who show symptoms of depression or excessive aggression, are helped to express themselves, to receive support and to integrate effectively with others.

The International Committee of the Red Cross (ICRC)

activities contribute immensely to the mental health of the minors by helping them *keep in touch with their families*. Messages between the children and their families are distributed by ICRC to families in accessible areas in southern Sudan, and this helps the children maintain some level of hope while they remain in refuge.

3.4 Documentation of Social History

The history of the unaccompanied children is collected through interviews with individual children by trained Sudanese interviewers. The objectives of the documentation exercise are to prepare information which can be used for *family tracing and reunification purposes* in the future, and to *preserve the children's life history*. It also provides an opportunity for each child to *express himself/herself* and to be listened to by an adult, to be consulted, and offered *special attention or affection* where appropriate. However, for a variety of reasons, including the continuing war and the practical difficulties in travelling in south Sudan, only limited work has been done to trace families.

The analysis and review of the data collected from the social history assists in the modification of the programmes for unaccompanied children through practical recommendations, and also in the development of knowledge of working with war affected children in the region, as is exemplified by the publication, "The Unaccompanied Minors of Southern Sudan"[13].

3.5 Primary and Secondary Education

These are core components of the psycho–social programme which seek to address the needs of the child in a structured learning environment. Through the schools programme, care–takers and teachers work together with regard to the performance and adjustment of children. An important aspect of the education programme is the *structure and routine* which it offers, and the emphasis placed on *psycho–social adjustment* and not just academic achievement. Teachers are offered training and support to enhance the development of a mental health care perspective in the entire programme.

An Education Policy, describing the aims and goals of education in the camp and spelling out codes of conduct for teachers, was drafted by the staff and the refugee community leaders. The purpose of the policy is to have clear objectives for the educational work in Kakuma. It is also an attempt by Rädda Barnen to involve refugees in taking a stronger role and responsibility for educating the youth in the refugee camp. The basic understanding is that the responsibility for educating the children lies with the refugee community itself, and that Rädda Barnen and the UNHCR should support but not replace the initiatives of the refugees.

The enrolment of girls in schools is very low, reportedly due to the unwillingness of parents and guardians to let girls walk to school alone and spend time with a lot of boys at school. The girls and women are also expected to cook for a growing number of adult males in the population, as it is considered demeaning for a Sudanese boy or man to be seen preparing food.

The refugees in the camp opted to base the school programme on the Kenyan curriculum in the schools. The local curriculum was adapted to include the history and geography of South Sudan, which was seen as important in helping the children to understand the background to the conflict and their own experiences and life in exile. However, the lack of trained teachers in the camp is a great constraint to the educational system.

4. Discussions and Analysis

4.1 The Evolving Approach to Psycho–social Programmes

Rädda Barnen's approach is seen as *adaptable and flexible* in order to accommodate specific changes in both the Pignudo and Kakuma refugee camps. The immediate needs in the camps and the socio–political conditions have had a direct impact on the work with refugees.

Rädda Barnen's partners in the work, the refugees, have come to understand the policies and objectives of Rädda Barnen as an impartial organisation which promotes the interests of children in difficult circumstances, regardless of race, religion or political affiliation. By extension, the refugees recognise the reasons for the work that Rädda Barnen wishes to accomplish.

The initial phase of the project concentrated on relief assistance and the treatment of mentally disturbed children in the Pignudo Refugee camp. Although efforts were made from the beginning to pay attention to anthropological issues, the *understanding of the culture of the people*, and the impact of this on the work in the refugee camp became stronger with the continued presence of Rädda Barnen.

The psycho–social intervention in Kakuma developed differently from that in Pignudo because of the following reasons:

- A split in the Sudan Peoples Liberation Movement (SPLM) resulted in a marked increase in the openness of the refugee community to outside influences and information sharing. More children started to discuss what they have gone through and their interest to be reunited with their families in Sudan, thereby submitting more accurate personal information which assists in family tracing and personal adjustment of the children.

- Another result of the split was the decreased control of the SPLM over the lives of the refugees. Although this has a positive impact on the protection of the children, some adult refugees suggest the potentially positive disciplining aspect resulting from a close connection with a political movement in guiding the lives of a large number of unaccompanied adolescents.

- The movement to Kakuma gave Rädda Barnen a chance to influence the improvement of psycho–social activities, based on the lessons learnt in Pignudo camp. One major change was the fostering of young children with families, and the organisation of the unaccompanied children in smaller groups.

- Most trained refugee workers from Pignudo arrived in Kakuma as refugees, thereby carrying out a continuation of their work. The continuity in relationships between the children and caretakers and teachers has clearly benefitted the children.

- There was also a major shift in Rädda Barnen's approach in Kakuma. This was particularly a growing emphasis on actively looking for *resources available in the refugee camp*, as opposed to an approach of focusing on what was missing.
- Rädda Barnen's policy of using the *UN Convention on the Rights of the Child* as a planning and monitoring tool was more effectively taken up by the field staff in 1992/93. This assisted in giving a theoretical and practical framework for the activities in the field.

Conditions and relationships in the refugee camp have continued to change, owing to the outcome of conflicts in Sudan, the split between political groups, and more immediate factors in the camp such as food distribution, scarcity of resources and arrival of large numbers of refugees. These changes need to be addressed with flexibility in planning and implementation. The social workers are therefore expected to be sensitive to changes and be able to predict consequences and act accordingly.

4.2 The Impact of the Programme on Children's Mental Health

Although the children in the refugee camp have gone through *repeated trauma and separation* from family members and friends, the incidence of mental disturbance reported was unexpectedly low. In Pignudo, *only about 1% of the population were identified as being functionally impaired* to the point where they could not cope adequately in their "homes" and in school. In Kakuma, the figure is now negligible, with no special care arrangements required. The overall very high level of school attendance and performance attest to the unexpectedly good adjustment of the large majority of children. Various factors in the culture and in the situation contributed to this result.

Rädda Barnen's psycho–social programmes were developed by putting the Sudanese children in the centre and aiming at promoting the *adjustment mechanisms that already exist in the culture and the prevailing social context*. The opportunity given traditionally for children to *administer themselves* and carry out responsibilities (such as tending cattle and giving priority to younger siblings in food/milk distribution in the cattle camps), is being promoted in the care-taking systems being developed in the refugee camps.

Since one of the major objectives of psycho–social programmes is to normalise the abnormal situation in the refugee camp, supplementary programmes which encourage the expression of ideas and feelings are devised. Cultural activities, such as *story telling, composing poems, recounting and discussing dreams, traditional songs and dancing* are organised by care–takers in the groups. The major ideas behind these functions and groupings are to serve as a means of *expressing emotions, understanding events, enhancing reconciliation and interactions* among members of different tribes and groups, all in ways that are culturally acceptable.

The Dinka, Nuer and the culture of the other tribes that are in the refugee camps generally promote the discussion and understanding of important social issues which resulted in children and adults having a clear and common understanding of the reason for their flight from their areas of origin. Indeed, *these issues are discussed thoroughly*, thereby resulting in better understanding of the problems and experiences of the war and a feeling of sharing the same problems. This is one of the major factors that have contributed to the adjustment of the unaccompanied minors in the refugee camps.

The *involvement of the refugee community* in the activities in the camp is supported in order to promote the feeling of the refugees that they have some control over their lives. One of the ways used by Rädda Barnen was to involve refugee leaders as an Advisory Group which are involved in the planning and implementation of activities in the camp.

The appropriateness of the activities to the culture and the needs in the community are frequently discussed with refugee leaders, and this helped to achieve sustainability of programmes from an early stage of the project. Special attention is given to the cost–effectiveness of the activities through joint planning and assessment of achievements.

4.3 "Pull" Factors and Work in the Area of Origin

The availability of better infrastructure and services in the refugee camp serves as a "pull" factor, which encourages children to leave Sudan and to remain in the refugee camp. As there are only three functioning secondary schools in southern Sudan, to receive children from around 1,000 primary schools, it is increasingly likely that primary school leavers will be attracted to Kakuma to join the secondary school. An effect of the imbalance of development can result in more children coming to the refugee camps in search of education.

The *extension of Rädda Barnen's work to cover some areas in Southern Sudan* showed that the refugee programme could significantly benefit from the work in the country of origin, both in terms of developing educational programmes and in planning for family reunification of unaccompanied children.

An information system is provided by UNICEF/Operation Lifeline Sudan (OLS), a cross–border operation of relief and rehabilitation for southern Sudan, of which 38 NGOs are members. As well as providing a forum for sharing experience, OLS is a help to Rädda Barnen in designing programmes that are appropriate in the area of origin, for example, in providing information on the education and training required to facilitate refugees' eventual reintegration into Sudan.

Such inputs enabled Rädda Barnen to build the capacity of the refugee workers to carry out the work of caring for war–affected children in the absence of Rädda Barnen. This was demonstrated in the performance of the refugee staff who carried out the planned activities during a six weeks long suspension of activities in the Kakuma refugee camp in 1994 which was prompted by a dispute between UNHCR and the refugee leaders.

169

4.4 Effect of "Institutionalisation"

The fact that unaccompanied children are targeted as priority for assistance has contributed to the development of a special group, entitled to special attention. Sometimes, children are heard to be referring to themselves as "Children of Rädda Barnen" or "Children of UNHCR", with decreased recognition of their responsibility to their community. It is important that, despite the unusual history and living situation of these young people, they should be helped to see themselves as *ordinary members of their own community*.

4.5 Changes in the Community

Although the refugee population in the camp is imbalanced, with women and children being the majority, and a marked gender imbalance amongst the children, representatives of all sectors of the Sudanese community are found, thereby making it function like a "complete" community, with its share of elders, traditional healers, chiefs, wise men, etc.

However, the length of time in refuge has resulted in a *weakening of the role of the family and traditional structures* such as traditional courts and traditional healers. The functioning of the traditional Sudanese community structure was observed to have been reduced in Kakuma as compared to Pignudo. The role of the community in educating the youth in their future adult roles has also decreased considerably. It was observed by the community leaders that the group of unaccompanied minors tended to be less obedient to the rules of their community.

The absence of the traditional initiation rites for adolescents is mentioned often as a major problem. A significant number of the population of the unaccompanied minors are growing from adolescence to youth, without the support of the traditional societal practices and relatively clear roles. Prostitution is reported to be on the increase in Kakuma town, which, of course, creates a high risk in the spread of HIV and other STDs.

But despite these constraints, a real sense of community exists within the camp, and this provides for the children both a *sense of belonging and communal identity*, and a *sense of security*, both of which have contributed substantially to their remarkable sense of well-being.

4.6 Refugee Participation

Planning and decision–making in collaboration with the refugee community has assisted in the development of a culture–sensitive approach. Most southern Sudanese communities, traditionally encourage and actively cultivate the abilities of children who show leadership qualities. This has given opportunity for Rädda Barnen to work with unaccompanied minors more effectively by *using older youngsters in leadership roles* than occurred in the refugee camp in Pignudo. Cultural practices are also taken into consideration when planning vocational training, education for girls, etc.

The approaches of the different aid agencies and donors to relief and development inputs aim at restoring the self–image of the refugees in everyday life. Refugees must be recognised as *responsible and productive individuals*, with potential for adjusting to a changing situation.

Activities in refugee camps need to be *integrated* so that the services are not just isolated services, but meaningful activities that contribute towards the normal life of the community members.

4.7 Staff Support

Although Rädda Barnen is a child–oriented organisation, it is clear that the child's needs can best be addressed in the cultural context, through integration with the needs of the community and the culture, and by working towards the meaningfulness of different activities in the refugee camp. Sometimes there is a need to work towards the coordination of activities with other agencies working in the same area.

The adult care-takers and teachers in the refugee camp were recruited without first being helped to solve their own personal problems. It was therefore found to be essential to plan *support programmes for the adults*, through training and counselling.

4.8 Protection

One of the major issues of discussion, over the years, in the refugee camps is the issue of protection of children against *recruitment into the war*. Although protection is the mandate of the UNHCR, Rädda Barnen's work involves discussion of the rights of children. One area of emphasis in such discussions with refugee staff is the right of a child not to be involved in any armed conflict. However, more work in disseminating the Convention on the Rights of the Child and in encouraging local protection measures is required.

The presence of Rädda Barnen in the camp, in itself, ensures the protection of children's rights to some extent. The daily contact of the staff with the unaccompanied children serves as one of the methods of advocacy. Staff are trained to identify, document and report problems with children.

The *education of girls* is another major issue, which requires a change of attitude within the community and the planning of appropriate educational approaches. One of the approaches being considered in Kakuma is to involve girls in adult education programmes and to decentralise educational facilities in order to improve the geographical accessibility of education to girls.

5. Conclusions

These unaccompanied children and youth have fared remarkably well considering the extent and frequency of the traumatic events, compounded by their experience of separation, that they have experienced, and despite the many constraints imposed by life in a refugee camp. The lack of symptoms which have been functionally impairing has been striking, with few signs of hatred, thoughts of revenge or debilitating depression. The major factors that contributed to the positive development of their mental health are based on the *traditional lifestyles and coping mechanisms* of the Sudanese community.

From the beginning of the exodus from Ethiopia, the refugees themselves have been active in *taking responsibility for themselves* and for the care of the unaccompanied children, with the efforts of external agencies seeking to support rather than to replace their efforts.

In Sudanese culture, children are expected – and taught how – to live in, and adjust to, the harsh conditions in the villages and cattle camps. The programmes implemented by Rädda Barnen have supplemented the functioning of such mechanisms. Care arrangements and preventive and curative mental health interventions are based on traditional practices and coping mechanisms. Western approaches have been avoided, while such traditional activities as story–telling, writing poems, discussing dreams and a range of other activities have been developed and adapted to meet the particular needs of the refugees.

Rädda Barnen's psycho–social programme can be seen not as a series of discrete activities but rather as an attempt to ensure that *all aspects of refugee life are integrated* – care arrangements, education, health programmes, interviewing and documenting the children's histories, personal support and a range of purposeful activities – in order to ensure an overall sense of well–being amongst this exceptionally large group of unaccompanied refugee children.

Psycho-social Care for Children with Refugee Background in Sweden: the Work of Rädda Barnen's Swedish Department

by Karin Edenhammar and Eva Larsson-Bellander

1. Background and Context

Sweden is a small country in the north of Europe with a population of 8.7 million. By tradition, it has had a relatively generous refugee policy which has meant that Sweden has received more refugees than any other country in Europe, relative to its population, in the last few years.

Sweden's reception of large refugee groups since the Second World War has been as follows:

- 121,000 refugees from the Nordic countries in connection with the Second World War, of which 60,000 were children evacuated from Finland, most of them returning later
- 45,000 refugees from the concentration camps in Germany after the Second World War
- 37,000 Kurds after the Islamic Revolution in Iran in 1979
- 35,000 Latin Americans fleeing political persecution during the 1970's

- 11,000 Eritreans fleeing the war there since the late 1960's
- 7,000 Somalis resulting from the unrest and civil war during the 1980's and 1990's
- 70,000 refugees from the former Yugoslavia since the outbreak of war in 1991

The numbers of people requesting asylum has fluctuated heavily in recent years, depending on world events, and during the present decade there have been policy changes making it increasingly difficult for refugees to be granted asylum.

From having been culturally homogeneous at the beginning of the present century, Sweden has now become a multi–cultural society.

The State and the Municipalities are jointly responsible for refugee reception. Most refugees are initially received at one of the reception centres and are then transferred to one of the Municipalities where accommodation is provided. In practice, refugees tend to be concentrated in particular areas, resulting in an unintended segregation of refugees from Swedish people. Integration in the areas of housing, employment and social interaction are acknowledged as a great problem for refugees.

With regard to educational provision, in some Municipalities, children are placed immediately into Swedish–speaking classes, while in others, special nurseries and classes are used to prepare children for the Swedish educational system.

This case study seeks to describe the range of approaches taken by Rädda Barnen in their work to help ensure that children with refugee and immigrant background[14] have the same rights and opportunities as Swedish children, and to consider the extent to which the wide variety of approaches adopted adequately addresses the range of needs which characterise refugee children in Sweden.

2. Methodologies Used in this Case Study

This study of Rädda Barnen's psycho–social work with children with a refugee background in Sweden is based on the following methodologies:

- *perusal of project descriptions*, booklets, reports, books and films
- direct *personal experience, observations* of current activities and *discussions* with key staff
- a *continuous dialogue* with people working directly with children with a refugee background

3. Policy for Rädda Barnen's Work for Children with Refugee Background

Rädda Barnen is a children's rights organisation working for the implementation of the UN Convention on the Rights of the Child.

The overall aim is that the rights of children affected by armed conflict and children with refugee background shall be respected in accordance with the UN Convention on the Rights of the Child. Rädda Barnen has drawn up a policy which requires that work shall result in:

- children with refugee background being *accorded the same rights* as other children in each respective country
- children who have experienced armed conflicts and political oppression being *rehabilitated*
- increasing *public consciousness* about the rights of the child
- preventing and making visible the *abuse of children* and supporting abused children

4. Rädda Barnen's Work with Children and Families with Refugee Background

Rädda Barnen has chosen to undertake, sometimes in partnership with other agencies, a range of projects designed to impact on some of the particular problems and issues facing refugee children and their families.

4.1 The Advisory Service for Asylum Seekers and Refugees

The objective of the Advisory Service, which is run jointly with the Swedish Refugee Council, the Swedish Church and Swedish Amnesty, is to increase legal rights for asylum seekers and refugees through the provision of advice, and to take steps to ensure that the UN Convention on the Rights of the Child is implemented in the asylum process. The Centre provides a central point where people can come for free advice. Priority is given to cases where children are involved, and support is given to promoting family reunion where possible.

4.2 The Centre for Children Affected by Armed Conflict

This Centre is part of Rädda Barnen's Centre for Children and Adolescents in Crisis, and accepts referrals in respect to children with difficult war and refugee experiences, both unaccompanied refugee children and children living with their families. Many of them will have experienced violence and fear, death, separation and loss, and some of the unaccompanied young people will be coping with a lack of adult support in their lives.

The competence to treat mental trauma among refugees has been developed at a considerably slower pace in Sweden than in many other countries. Only recently has crisis preparedness become a feature of psychiatric care. The treatment of those who have suffered injuries by torture and war still takes place mainly outside of the established area of psychiatry. The statutory Child and Adolescent Psychiatry Services found themselves to be relatively unprepared for such problems, and have had to develop appropriate means of treating family groups and individual members of the family, for example by using crisis intervention techniques and making use of the family's healthy resources.

The Centre for Children Affected by Armed Conflict has developed psychoanalytical approaches to working with individual children (including very small children) and adolescents and families using individual and family therapy, art and play therapy. Most of the work is undertaken through interpreters.

An important aspect of this clinical work is the collection of knowledge about the effects of war on children and about different approaches to assisting them. Study of the current literature and exchange of experience with other centres are also important aspects of the work.

4.3 Drama, Classical Music and Dance Workshops for Refugee Children

The arrival of many refugees from Bosnia in the early '90s prompted the need to promote preventive activities for refugee children. Experience indicates that people who can make use of their imagination and creativity can endure difficult situations more effectively than others. Creative activities help people to express themselves, to facilitate adaptation to new situations and enable people to go on living with difficult situations. All of these can, in turn, increase their quality of life.

The drama, classical music and dance workshops have been going on for three years and during this time, working methods have been developing constantly. In the beginning, the work took place in the refugee reception centres, but was subsequently developed in ordinary pre–schools and schools where most of the refugee children can be found. The workshops have been of great help to the teachers as well as to the children themselves. This work has been documented in reports, video films and books.

The dance workshops give children an opportunity to see themselves and others without using words. Before young children learn to speak, they express themselves by movement: in dance, children's need of play and movement, and the non–verbal communication it involves, can be utilised. This gives refugee children an opportunity to meet their classmates at the same level, and at the same time, they have an outlet for their emotional blockages. Through the medium of dance, they can learn to relax, express themselves spontaneously, and learn to make contact with other people. Some children, for example, those facing considerable difficulties and tensions in the classroom, find that they can relax, enjoy and make progress in the dance workshops.

The drama workshops provide children with opportunities to explore relationships between people, both playfully and seriously. Methods are used which strengthen the ability of children to live the part being played, thereby increasing the understanding of other human beings.

These workshops provide opportunities for exploring difficult and painful issues such as flight, the experience of becoming a refugee, loss, ethnicity and culture, returning home etc., sometimes using relatively "safe" exercises such as "going on holiday". The aim is to use a variety of different methods involving mime, games in small and large groups, playlets etc., all in an atmosphere of relaxation and enjoyment. Through these means, children can begin to express themselves and explore their thoughts and experiences which can help them to adjust to their current situation.

In the *classical music workshops*, an emotional–educational method is used. Classical music has the potential for evoking a wide range of emotions, and children can learn to differentiate and recognise different feelings such as sadness, grief, fear and happiness. They can also show such feelings in movement and painting.

By tradition classical music has been considered to be reserved for adults. However, classical music can be the basis of pre–school children's greater ability to understand and express feelings – e.g.

certain music makes them think of certain stories and situations. Pieces by well–known composers such as Grieg and Britten are used in the work.

A pedagogic method has been developed, as an initiative by a private agency, and used in the training of 400 teachers, and over 3,000 children have participated in the activities. This method was then developed more specifically for children with refugee background in either special classes or integrated with other children. To date about 80 pre–school and school teachers have received this more specialised training, with the methodology continuously developing as the growing potential of this dynamic way of working is realised.

With all of these different workshops, maximum impact is probably achieved where the workshop leaders are able to integrate their work with that of the school teachers, for example in working on particular issues raised in class and enabling teachers to continue to work on these issues, and in involving teachers themselves in developing new means of communication in the class.

4.4 Voluntary Work in the Local Societies

Rädda Barnen is organised in 300 local societies all over Sweden and has a total membership of 80,000 people, some of whom support and work voluntarily for the organisation.

Some 120 members have volunteered to take on responsibility for refugee matters. This contact network is an invaluable help in the work of spreading information about refugee matters amongst the membership, and in providing means of monitoring the refugee situation and taking action in the local area.

These volunteers are working in a variety of areas: for example, with study circles with refugee women which deal with issues of bringing up children, sewing groups and running cafes in reception centres, in which both adults and children are welcome. Rädda Barnen also has voluntary representatives in schools, where the work has been mainly directed towards international issues.

Rädda Barnen recruits volunteers to act as *legal guardians* for unaccompanied refugee children, and assist staff in refugee centres in arranging outings, get–togethers and in helping children with homework. Members are also beginning to take on important roles in *befriending* refugee children. For example, Rädda Barnen is identifying an appropriate contact–person for individual unaccompanied refugee children, to provide support, help in developing cultural competence and so on. Support for volunteers engaged in this work is provided.

5. Rädda Barnen's Work in a Wider Community Context

As a children's rights organisation, Rädda Barnen has been increasingly concerned about having impact on policies, professional practices, public attitudes and legislation in order to achieve improvements for children with refugee background. Experience from Rädda Barnen's own direct work with children and families is often the basis for actions in these areas.

5.1 Policy and Advocacy Work

Rädda Barnen collaborates with the Swedish Network of Parliamentarians for Children's Rights, a network aiming to monitor children's rights. It has regular meetings with this Network, and in this way it has an opportunity to suggest legislative changes required to make improvements for children with refugee background.

This group was the host of a conference on the subject "Is Sweden Failing the Refugee Children?" which was held at the Swedish Parliament. Rädda Barnen's experience, knowledge and ideas for improvements were gathered in a report under the same title. Rädda Barnen's demands include the following:

• that all children with refugee background in Sweden receive the *same health, hospital and dental care* that Swedish children receive, even those applying for residence permits for reasons other than asylum;

- that all children with refugee background, regardless of whether they have a residence permit, shall have the right to *adequate physical, mental and social rehabilitation;*
- that *each child shall be heard in the investigation* which is made concerning the child's right to a residence permit. The child shall be heard by staff with adequate education and knowledge of children.

During 1994, Sweden faced the issues posed by the large numbers of refugees arriving from the former Yugoslavia. To draw attention to the needs of these children, Rädda Barnen held a number of seminars around the country in 1994: these addressed local authority decision–makers, schools and social services staff, involving about 3,000 people altogether.

Rädda Barnen is constantly working to make information available concerning children with refugee background in the form of reports, booklets and books as well as participation in seminars. It is also participating in various networks and short–term reference groups concerning refugee questions: these involve both legal and psycho–social issues, and take place on both national and international levels.

5.2 Training for Pre–School Workers: Child Care in a Multi–Cultural Society

During the last three years, Rädda Barnen has been working with training and methodology development for pre–school child care workers in seven different communities in Sweden to prepare pedagogues for working in an international society with children from different parts of the world, some of whom have had very difficult experiences.

The rationale behind this project is that all children in Sweden are going to live in a society that will become more and more internationalised and culturally heterogeneous. Pre–schools are places where children can receive help to prepare themselves for life in an increasingly international society. The *project helps to develop an anti-racist profile*, to actively fight prejudice and discrimination and to work for a more tolerant, multi-cultural society irrespective of the actual ethnic composition of particular pre-schools. It has become apparent that a conscious, clear and goal-oriented pedagogic way of working is a prerequisite for child care workers who want to work for solidarity, internationalism and anti-racism.

The project will be concluded during the autumn of 1995 and a book will be published which can be used by everybody working with children. It has, as its starting point, the UN Convention on the Rights of the Child, and its main emphasis is on people's capacity for insight and empathy towards both children and adults.

The aim of the project has been to convey knowledge, support and guidance to child care workers about the situation of children with refugee background, in order to complement the efforts of the communities and other NGOs. The goal has been to make child care workers aware of their own attitudes towards the children and how they themselves can develop a way of working that is tolerant and understanding in all everyday situations. In the long run this can help to counteract discrimination and xenophobia.

Guidance, seminars, study circles and study days have been concentrated on certain areas and groups in order to try to achieve a balance between getting wide experience from different areas and in-depth experience from a few chosen areas.

5.3 The Rädda Barnen Cup

Rädda Barnen has sponsored a football competition for young people aged 13–15. Young people from different cultures are encouraged to play football together as a means of bringing them into more personal contact with each other to *counteract xenophobia, racism and discrimination.* Training in conflict resolution and mediation for these youths is also a part of the project. The idea is that they then act as ambassadors in their schools to initiate discussions on ways of further developing the work against xenophobia and racism.

5.4 Continuing Education for Professional Workers

There is a great demand for Rädda Barnen to contribute to the continuing education of child care workers, teachers and others in areas in which Rädda Barnen has been involved over the years. These areas include children with refugee background, children affected by armed conflict, children experiencing mourning and loss, and the Convention on the Rights of the Child. For many years the Swedish Department has been arranging seminars and lectures during the "Children's Days" which are events organised for a wide variety of professionals working with children and youth.

Rädda Barnen also offers educational "packages" for local authorities and various other organisations, which are held in Stockholm and other venues throughout the country. Such events, along with Rädda Barnen's published reports, books and booklets, provide opportunities to disseminate the ideas and the knowledge that Rädda Barnen has gathered. This educative work also provides continuous knowledge and invaluable dialogue regarding the conditions of refugee children in Sweden.

5.5 Research into Unaccompanied African Children

Rädda Barnen's Centre for Children Affected by Armed Conflict and the Advisory Service for Asylum Seekers and Refugees have both observed that the most vulnerable group among the refugee children in Sweden is that of the unaccompanied minors from Africa. Since 1989 approximately 500 African children have arrived without a legal guardian.

In order to improve the reception and care of these children, Rädda Barnen has started a research project to find out more about the situation of unaccompanied African children in Sweden. As well as analysing existing statistical information, the project involves interviewing individuals in order to "give children a voice" and talk about their experiences in their country of origin, during flight, their arrival in Sweden, their current situation and hopes and fears for the future.

Although this research is still progressing, initial results from the interviews paint a depressing picture of the *extremely difficult situation facing many of these young people*. The themes of false hopes and failed expectations emerge clearly. In particular, the following points seem to be most significant:

- Many face a profound sense of *loneliness and isolation*: they miss their own families, have no friends and little contact with Swedish people
- They experience *difficulty in adjusting* to the expected patterns of behaviour in Sweden, especially with regard to authority issues
- Many have experienced great *difficulties in being reunited with their families*
- Many were experiencing *difficulties in school*, with language difficulties, limited previous experience of, and different attitudes towards education
- *Anxieties about the future* were very common: school failure, lack of confidence about finding work, segregation and isolation, and total dependence on society, were common themes.
- Some were so miserable that they would consider *returning to their original country*.

These provisional findings clearly pose many challenges to organisations concerned with refugee children, and will be discussed further in para. 6.2 below.

6. Discussion and Analysis

6.1 The Evolution and Scope of Rädda Barnen's Programme

Rädda Barnen's work with refugee children has evolved into a pattern which seeks to intervene in a *variety of ways and on a variety of levels*. From an initial orientation based on the mainly psychological background of staff, it has evolved into a very diverse programme adopting quite different approaches: these range from work with individual children and their families (Advice Centre, Centre for Children Affected by Armed Conflict) to preventive work (dance, drama and music workshops); from professional education and training to policy and advocacy work; from addressing problems of racism and xenophobia through the training of pre–school staff to voluntary work by local associations.

Central to this diverse range of activities is the importance of *developing and disseminating knowledge of the problems and needs of refugee children*. This growing body of knowledge and experience enables Rädda Barnen both to seek to influence policy, legislation, practice and public opinion, and also to continue to develop and change its own programme. The current research into the situation of Unaccompanied African Refugee Children is a good example of a piece of work which is likely to have a significant impact, and raises a number of important questions. In particular, it may prompt Rädda Barnen and other agencies to reconsider how refugee children are supported within their communities, whether more needs to be done to address community attitudes towards immigrants, and whether the difficult question of voluntary return needs to be reconsidered.

6.2 The Integration of Refugees into Swedish Life

As indicated in the introduction to this case study, Sweden has traditionally adopted a very welcoming attitude to those seeking refuge and asylum. However, behind this fact lie a great deal of problems facing refugees in adjusting to a society which, though having become increasingly multi–cultural, nevertheless is not taking appropriate measures to meet the consequences of this changed situation.

Society must give all refugees an *opportunity to participate* in the working life and in political decision–making. Today refugees are under–represented at all levels in society except within the ranks of the unemployed. The different refugee groups live in separate housing areas, mainly near big cities, despite the aim of refugees being received in all local authority areas.

Many individual refugees say that they *live lives isolated from Swedish people*, and this has been confirmed in many investigations and was especially highlighted in the preliminary findings of Rädda Barnen's research into the situation of African Unaccompanied Refugee Children. Many have no contact with Swedish children, and in some areas there are no Swedish children in the pre–schools and schools. Many refugee children express a great *loneliness and a longing for Swedish friends*. In particular, adolescents look upon themselves as losers and feel themselves to be outsiders. They believe that their chances of getting a job are small and amongst some groups the unemployment rate is as high as 90%. This group is over–represented when it comes to crime.

It was partly in response to these problems that Rädda Barnen decided to focus on preventive work in pre–schools as a means of impacting, at an early and formative stage in people's lives, on the attitudinal problems that lie behind racism, discrimination and xenophobia. The Rädda Barnen Cup was also initiated in order to address these attitudes among young people.

6.3. The Need to Improve Community Support for Refugees

In Sweden there is little familiarity with the idea of voluntary work and it has therefore been difficult to find ways of working with refugees on a voluntary, befriending basis. Swedish society has, until comparatively recently, been a fairly homogeneous society and many Swedes are not used to having contact with refugees from other cultures. Rädda Barnen recognises the need for the whole society to take appropriate measures to improve the community support for refugees. There is also a clear need to further develop the befriending work, both by *involving volunteers*, and by *encouraging meeting points* between people with different cultural backgrounds. It is also recognised that members of different cultural groups also need to be more centrally involved in Rädda Barnen's planning, and there may be scope for supporting refugees' own groups and networks.

6.4 Responding to the Needs of Children Psychologically Affected by War

As already indicated, the Rädda Barnen Centre for Children Affected by Armed Conflict serves an important function in obtaining knowledge which, in turn, informs other areas of work. An awareness of the effects of traumatic experience on the youngest children has begun to be developed only during the last few years. The youngest children coming to the Centre have all been affected by severe trauma, which without help would continue to seriously affect their mental health and further development. If this work can start in time, the prognosis is good, but there is a need to develop other methods to assist mothers and children.

One theme to emerge from this clinical experience is the *link between political violence and violence within the family*. Families from Bosnia, for example, sometimes illustrate the way in which ethnic violence within communities has created considerable intra–family tensions and difficulties.

One challenge for the Centre is to develop approaches which may enable them to reach larger numbers of children, perhaps by using time–limited treatment methods. Another is for the staff working in this Centre to spread their expertise beyond the confines of the clinic. Recently a group of staff from the Centre have become involved in the training of professional workers in the former Yugoslavia, and in sharing the experience of working with children and families who have experienced war and displacement.

The knowledge that many children with a refugee background have had difficult experiences of war and flight has made it necessary for Rädda Barnen to develop pedagogic methods to reach these substantial numbers of children. These are often mentally healthy children not requiring clinical help but who nevertheless have experienced and witnessed extreme violence – i.e. they are *normal children who have reacted to abnormal situations*. Methods have been chosen which need no words (e.g. drama, dance and music) as many of these children speak little or no Swedish. It has also been shown that approaches which are enjoyable make it easier for children to work at their more difficult experiences. Happy and enjoyable experiences in these activities make it easier to learn, the key to further development. These activities arouse the curiosity of the children and give them the opportunity to generate new energy. Such approaches need to continue to be developed: new creative methods need to be found, and Rädda Barnen wants to reach as many refugee children as possible through such means.

7. Conclusions

Rädda Barnen's work with refugees and asylum seekers in Sweden can be seen as a developing process which has tried to take a *holistic perspective by working with a wide variety of methods, and on a range of different levels*. Rädda Barnen have chosen to work with individual children, with families, in pre–schools and schools, with a wide variety of professionals, in the wider community, and by impacting on the policy and legislation level through advocacy and lobbying. By retaining direct involvement with refugees through such means as its clinic and advisory work, it has continued to develop its knowledge of refugees, and of the ever–changing pattern of problems and needs that they bring to Sweden.

This evolving knowledge has been supplemented by specific re-search programmes and contact with other professionals. In turn this knowledge has informed its work which aims to impact on policy, legislation and practice through advocacy, professional education and publications.

The research into the situation of African Unaccompanied Children in Sweden paints a very *pessimistic picture which is prompting a radical reappraisal* of the way in which unaccompanied children are supported and helped, and it raises the emotive issue of voluntary return to the country of origin. The research serves as a powerful reminder that there is still a long way to go to ensure that children with refugee background have the same rights as other children under the UN Convention on the Rights of the Child.

"Contamination by War: Strategies for Restoration by Collective Action"

by Eva Segerström

1. Background and Context

Most of the Somali refugees who fled to Yemen during the spring and summer of 1992 crossed the Sea of Aden and ended up in Medinat Al Shaab refugee camp in a sandy desert 10 km. From the city of Aden. The camp environment had few facilities apart from a food distribution system and a small health clinic.

Rädda Barnen had been working in Yemen for the previous 30 years, primarily in the field of primary health, and as one of the few NGOs working there, took the initiative to plan and start a primary school in the camp. It was immediately apparent that many of the children and their parents had had experiences of violence and other traumatic events in Somalia which were compounded by the current stresses and absence of support in the refugee camp. Six months later, a survey was undertaken to assess the psychological well–being of refugee mothers, and to evaluate their competence to meet the needs of their children. As a result of this survey, ideas were formulated on ways to improve the mothers' sense of psychological well–being and parental competence by encouraging their active participation in a range of community development activities.

The initiation of the school and work with women in the camp were seen as the two main aspects of a strategy adopted by Rädda Barnen to promote the psychological recovery and social integration of Somali refugee children in Yemen. The aim of the school was not just to provide education in a traditional manner, but also to provide training for teachers in order to enable them to assess the psychological needs of children, to provide social support to them through supportive conversations, and to encourage their participation in cultural activities such as music, dance and drama.

This case study examines these two aspects of Rädda Barnen's strategy to impact on the psycho–social well–being of the children. The implementation of the strategy was, however, impeded by two major factors.

First, the refugees experienced several moves, and the extreme disruption created by the outbreak of civil war in Yemen. After suffering further traumatising experiences through being caught up in this war and the need to flee the refugee camp, they were eventually resettled in Algahin, which is situated in a barren, rocky area two hours' drive from Aden.

Second, for various operational reasons apart from these disruptions, it was not possible for Rädda Barnen to provide the level and consistency of professional support which these programmes really needed. Although the school received good technical support in the form of various teacher training modules, it was not possible to provide social work input into the Women's Union. However, when in the spring of 1995 the writer, who was involved in setting up the programmes, was able to revisit the refugees in the new camp in Algahin, the information which emerged provided some interesting and unexpected findings, which will be described in this case study.

After a brief section outlining the methodologies used in compiling the study, a description of the development of the school will be offered, along with an picture of what was encountered during the return visit in 1995. This will be followed by an account of the survey of women in the camp which was undertaken in 1993, and an explanation of the developments which occurred as a result of this. Following a section which discusses and analyses some of the main issues arising from the development of these two programmes, some conclusions will be drawn.

2. Methodologies Used in Compiling this Case Study

This study is based both on the original work undertaken in setting up the two programmes in Yemen (including the survey of women in the camp[15]) and on the findings when the refugees were revisited in 1995. On this latter occasion, the following methodologies were used:

- *Semi–structured interviews* with key individuals within the refugee camp, the Women's Association and the school
- *Focus–group discussions* with mothers, children and camp leaders
- A *participatory review* with teachers in the school to provide opportunities for more structured discussion of the events within the school and their impact on the life of the community
- *Observation of activities* within the refugee camp: these involved teachers, parents, women and children

3. The Planning and Development of the School

3.1 The Planning of the School

The school started in November 1992 after one month's planning and preparation. The first step was to establish an Education Committee comprising refugees selected by the community. The Committee eventually consisted of seven men and three women, chosen from different tribes (seen as vital in a society deeply divided along tribal lines) and from different zones in the camp. The planning of the school was based on a clear statement of community–development principles, which included the following:

the approach should be *collective*, within and with the refugee community; the *community should define needs and objectives*; *resources should come from within the community*, supported where needed by external ones; decision–making should be *democratic*. It was also decided that the approach should aim to meet the *broader psycho–social needs* of children.

Much of the planning was undertaken by the *Education Committee*, working largely without representation of Rädda Barnen staff. Rädda Barnen was, however, requested to take an active role in *teacher selection* to prevent suspicion of tribal preferences, though the final selection was made jointly. Rädda Barnen determined that only modest salaries should be paid. Only teachers who expressed a more altruistic motive were considered – i.e. those who wanted to work for children and not those motivated by material rewards or the need for "something to do". Another criterion was the capacity to deal with the children in difficult situations: only teachers who expressed a wish to understand the child, to avoid physical punishment and to find constructive approaches were appointed. When the school started, there was one head–teacher, 10 teachers and 450 children aged from 6 to 9 years of age.

Early discussions with the teachers revealed the general view that "it is best for children not to talk about the bad experiences they have gone through even though sometimes children want to talk about them". This suggested the existence of a *taboo against discussing painful issues*, and from this it seemed that there was a need for knowledge and awareness of psychological concepts. It was therefore recommended that it was necessary to include, in the subjects for teacher training, the knowledge and skills required for offering "supportive talks" with children to give them help, advice and emotional support in their daily lives.

3.2 The School in Algahin, Two Years Later

When the return visit was made in 1995, it was found that the camp consisted of nine huge hangars, one of which was used as the school and also for food distribution. In spite of the extreme hardship the refugees had experienced prior to their resettlement in Algahin, the group of teachers had immediately re–established the school.

The school comprised a pre–school and primary school, with a total of 16 teachers, including two female pre–school teachers, a headmaster and deputy. Most had been involved in the school since its inception. There were 507 children enrolled, of whom 211 were girls. Owing to the civil war in Yemen, no textbooks were available.

First impressions suggested a traditional school with traditional teaching methods – i.e. teachers operating in a "top–down" relationship using a very formal and non–interactive approach, which included the use of repetition as a learning method. But in other respects the school was found to be exceptional. The deputy headmaster made a very significant comment:

> The school is not just a school for education:it is a community school.

The school had become the main social structure within the camp and the most important community service available. The camp was found to lack an official and united camp committee – rather a number of leaders represented different tribes within the community but did not speak with one voice on behalf of the whole community. However, mutual respect between the elders and the teachers' group was clearly seen to exist.

When the school started, the Education Committee had a central role, but by the time of the return visit in 1995 it was found to have been disbanded because of conflicts of interest. The headteacher and his staff formed a self–steering, independent unit which was considered by the teachers to be an clear strength.

During this return visit, a participatory review was undertaken with the school staff in order to provide a structured way of analysing the way in which the school had developed. The following are some of the key issues to emerge from this review:

- All teachers valued their *involvement in discussions and decisions* concerning the school. The teachers committed a great deal of time to discussing issues, and though the headmaster would make final decisions it was always on the basis of thorough discussion.

- *Cooperation with parents was referred to as partnership*: parents were actively involved in communicating with them regarding progress and behaviour. Teachers knew the parents and the family background of the children. School staff were also *involved with issues beyond the confines of the school*. They were, for example, consulted in matters such as arranging celebrations and activities, dealing with inter–personal conflicts etc. During the visit, a group of eight parents voluntarily assisted in the construction of a storehouse for the school, complete with furniture, working until late at night to complete their task.
- The teachers showed a great deal of interest and knowledge in *recognising and assessing stress in children*, including gender differences and the need to recognise the problems displayed by children who failed to attend school or who were sad and silent.
- *Teachers' responses to children who were troubled by their difficult experiences* included the following:
  - they *discussed the problem with parents*
  - the children would be given *extra attention* in class
  - teachers would *encourage the child with hobbies and interests*
  - *other children would be encouraged to help and support the child*
  - the child would be *encouraged to read the Koran* and listen to music
- It was significant that, contrary to what had been intended when the school was established, *teachers were generally reluctant to talk directly with the children about war experiences*, though some would have individual discussions with children when they themselves showed the desire to talk. However, it was clear that in activities such as singing, drama and free drawing, experiences of war and children's reactions to them were expressed.
- The teachers themselves adopted a number of strategies for *dealing with their own difficult experiences*. These included

reciting the Koran and developing their faith, learning more through reading and listening to the radio and taking part in a range of different activities.

- Teachers had become *involved in a wide range of activities within the wider community. Boy Scouts and Girl Guides* groups were established to teach good social values, social awareness, discipline and self reliance, and to involve children as active participants in community development programmes. A *"Children's Corner"* was established to provide a forum for various out–of–school activities, including story–telling, plays, singing, quizzes etc.. These took place at various times during the week, with parents also involved in two of the weekly sessions. One teacher expressed a major function of the Children's Corner thus: "Teachers will present different stories that touch on aspects of real life. This will help the teachers to draw out the child's emotions of happiness and sadness". Another important objective was to develop *clear forms of communiction* with other children, with parents and within the wider community. *Sports activities* were also organised by the teachers, including football and volley–ball teams.
- Teachers had also *involved themselves in a number of other activities* which contain: translating useful written material from English into Somali, evaluating the school's performance and reviewing the curriculum, undertaking case studies (e.g. on why there fewer girls aged 12–15 than boys in the school, and on children and who are affected by their experiences of war), and planning publications (including a school paper to include writings on various topics).

This wide range of activities illustrates both the enthusiasm and commitment of the teachers and their desire to be involved in the lives of the children, their families and in the wider community on a much broader basis than is typical of the traditional role of the teacher. The particular approach taken in responding to the needs of children psychologically affected by their experiences of war will be discussed further in section 5 below.

4. Description of the Programme Planned for Women

4.1 Previous Research

It is well known that mothers' emotional well–being is important for their children's psychological health and development. Recent research indicates that young children can cope well with the stress of social disasters like war if they retain strong attachment to their families, and if parents can continue to project a sense of stability, permanence and competence to their children[16]. In this sense, parents can enhance the *resilience* of their children by mediating between their difficult experiences and their sense of well–being. Research also suggested that if mothers themselves receive good social support, this is likely to reduce their levels of stress related to traumatic events. These findings were the basis for a survey of 198 mothers made in Medinat Al Shaab in May 1993. How was the Somali refugee mothers' psychological well–being and their sense of competence to care for their children? The study was made not just out of theoretical interest, but in order to place emphasis on mothers and the central role they should have in any programmes planned in the camp.

4.2 The Survey in Medinal Al Shaab

The survey showed that the refugee *mothers' psychological well–being was very poor*. Half of the mothers interviewed expressed an extremely high degree of psychosomatic and emotional problems, while only 2% had no, or very few, symptoms. A majority (85%) suffered daily from different stress factors to an extreme degree. About 20% of the mothers had been exposed to many traumatic events, half to some such events, with only 3.5% having had little or no exposure to traumatic events. About 90% of the mothers expressed feelings of helplessness about bringing up their own children. A similar proportion considered themselves as being the most important person for the child. About 40% of the mothers received support from husbands, but most said that they have nobody giving emotional support.

4.3 Enhancing Maternal Support to their Children

All children, and especially those affected by war, need a daily structure and routine. The camp school provided an important part of this structure and became the first community service for children. But what could be done to increase the mothers' sense of competence to enable them to be more supportive to their children?

As a result of the survey, a strategy to empower women was devised. Some of the women had organised themselves into a *Women's Union* and they requested donor organisations to assist by providing a *meeting centre* for all women in the camp where they could discuss issues of interest and concern to themselves. This proposal was consistent with McCallin and Fozzard's conclusion[17] that an effective means of support was to *strengthen women's social networks*, which can be seen as a protective factor, and increase their participation in the community. This in turn should result in a greater sense of control over their lives and a diminished sense of helplessness. The result is an increase in resilience both for women and for their children.

4.4 The Women's Union and Subsequent Developments

In the Medinat Al Shaab camp, a meeting place was duly provided and the women began to regain control of their lives through the dynamics and resilience of the Women's Union which was becoming an important resource for women and children. Various interest groups were set up, including ones to concentrate on hygiene and health care, education and child care, social and cultural activities and home economics, conflict resolution, and help to people in need. After the camp moved for the first time, the group again was provided with a place to meet, but the activities appear to have been limited to handicrafts and literacy classes. At the time of the follow–up visit to Algahin, the Women's Union had been re–established, but its *apparent lack of impact on the life of women in the camp was disappointing.* It had ceased to be a democratic organisation, leadership being concentrated in the hands of one very authoritarian person. Its lack of commitment to community development was illustrated by the demand that an institution should be opened for all the orphans currently cared for by their relatives. The Union had become little more than a place for women to meet and undertake a limited range of activities. The various sub–groups no longer existed and the Union had lost its concern for child health, play, and the broader pursuit of women's issues in the community. Why was this, when the Women's Union seemed to have the potential for becoming an extremely important resource for women?

One reason appeared to be the *lack of leadership* which was needed for the Union to develop in a committed and imaginative manner. Many of the more influential female leaders in the camp left, and were replaced in the Women's Union by self–elected women who had more interest in financial benefits than the good of the whole community.

A second reason is probably that women seem to associate and socialise mainly in *small informal groups* rather in large, visible, well–structured organisations. At the time of the follow–up visit, it was noticeable that about half of the small businesses in the market place were run by women – tea–shops, market stalls etc.. Moreover, the majority of mothers were spontaneously and informally meeting other mothers (especially those with small children) in small groups, or they were busily occupied in the traditional activity of running the home.

5. Discussion and Analysis

The school was observed to be operating with an amazing level of *enthusiasm and commitment,* despite the experience of two wars, repeated displacement, the very poor physical environment of the camp and the lack of teaching materials. The teachers give much of the credit for this to the management and leadership in the school, though the recruitment of effective and devoted teachers who had a high commitment to the children was also a very significant factor. Personality attributes were a more important selection criterion than experience of teaching. The approach to the planning of the school was also extremely important. The people themselves took responsibility for defining needs, taking decisions collectively and planning the school. Given the tribal nature of the conflict in Somalia, the recruitment of members of the Education Committee, and of the teachers themselves, from different tribal groups was significant. This enabled a *participative ethos* to develop in the school, in which all teachers felt themselves to be involved in decisions. This resulted in a strong sense of ownership of what they were doing, coupled with an equally strong sense of responsibility to the community as a whole.

Despite the fact that the teachers adopted the traditional educational methods which are typical of the culture, outside of the classroom situation their role *evolved in a flexible and non–conventional manner*, extending their work and influence out into the community. This broadening of their role partly reflected the broad range of teacher training modules provided by Rädda Barnen.

Many factors are important in working to promote the psychological well–being of refugee children. Undoubtedly the most important factor for the child is to belong to a family and a community, both of which can serve to rebuild a sense of stability and security and thereby enhance their resilience. A *social environment of care and support promotes both health and psychological recovery*, and this is just what the teachers' group show in action. They also demonstrate that it is possible not just to run a school, but to do so in a way that makes the school the most influential and stable community resource.

It has to be admitted that the school was not consciously planned in quite this way, and the return visit in 1995 showed that all expectations of what the school could achieve had been exceeded. In the context of a refugee camp lacking a strong and united leadership structure, the teachers' group took this role, becoming respected leaders within the community. The sense of partnership with parents also helped to raise their status and enhance their role vis à vis families in the camp.

By way of contrast, the high hopes of an effective and dynamic Women's Union did not materialise. Just as the school became successful partly as a reflection of good leadership, the Women's Union failed partly because of the lack of good leadership, a problem which seems to have been compounded by the assumption that once established, it would develop through its own internal resources. With hindsight, it seems that the women *needed more facilitative support during the early implementation stage.* Greater clarity of aims and a stronger sense of ownership by the women themselves probably required longer–term support by external personnel with sound knowledge and experience of community work practice and principles: this Rädda Barnen, for various reasons, could not provide.

But a second reason has also been suggested, that perhaps Somali women are more familiar with a pattern of social interaction that is more informal and occurs in small groups. With hindsight, perhaps the vision for the Women's Union was too ambitious. It might have been more appropriate to begin with the more immediate life–tasks facing Somali women – giving birth, feeding and caring for children, looking after the home and perhaps engaging in modest business enterprises. Instead of trying to support the more formal leadership patterns required by a social organisation such as a Women's Union, it might have been more appropriate to work to *identify the less visible patterns of informal leadership* amongst the women in the camp, and find ways to support and strengthen these. Given the lack of the more formal, more visible patterns of leadership among the women in Algahin, the leadership of the Women's Union was likely to depend on a small number of powerful women, leaving the Union vulnerable to inappropriate and autocratic leadership.

Perhaps the most interesting issue to emerge from the follow–up visit was the manner in which the school teachers had approached the psychological needs of the children. The original intention was to introduce a substantial element of psychological knowledge into the training of teachers to enable them not only to recognise the symptoms of stress in children, but to be able to respond to them through individual and group discussions about their experiences and the impact of them in their lives.

In the follow–up visit in 1995, it was revealed that the intended training in psycho–social needs had not been undertaken, for a variety of reasons. It was equally clear that the teachers' group had a *very clear concept of children's psycho–social needs*, though terms such as this were not actually used. But rather than pursuing the idea of group discussions in school about difficult experiences, and the idea of "supportive conversations" with individual children, the school staff had *evolved their own methods* of working purposefully with the children. These methods emphasised patterns of communication and expression other than verbal interaction which Western approaches tend to stress. They had placed particular emphasis on the importance of *daily structure, adult support and play* in promoting the psycho–social well–being of the children, and these were very evident in the various activities planned and implemented by the teachers. They had taken their role outside of the school, first in *promoting partnership with parents*, and also in developing a wide range of *out–of–school activities*. Rather than seeing reactions to traumatic experiences as individual problems, they preferred rather to emphasise that everyone in the camp has experienced violence, war and displacement, and that the whole community is not only grieving together but also *coping collectively*.

Community–building is a way for adults to cope with difficult experiences, a collective coping strategy. The teachers expressed this by saying that they deal with difficult experiences by such means as "taking part", "creating", "learning more" and by "maintaining a strong belief in God". To *belong to a well–functioning community* where there are strong ties between its members, may be the most important coping strategy.

6. Conclusions

This group of Somali refugees had been not only traumatised by their experiences of war and displacement in their own country, but had to contend with a move to another site in Yemen and finally the experience of being caught up in a war in the country of refuge, and the consequent sense of retraumatisation and further displacement. Furthermore, the camp environment was far from satisfactory, located in a barren area with a harsh climate.

In the face of all these difficulties, and with only minimal external assistance, the school re–established itself, and at the time of the return visit offered a *vibrant resource to the children and to the whole community*. A high sense of morale existed among the school staff, reflecting various factors, including excellent leadership, the participative manner in which the school was first developed, and the support and training provided by Rädda Barnen. In contrast, the idea of the Women's Union did not really develop as was orignally envisaged. As an organisation it failed because of the absence of some of the factors which enabled the school to succeed. With the benefits of hindsight, it now seems clear that more should have been done to identify the less visible, small–scale leadership patterns already existing amongst the women of the camp, and support these rather than promoting a more formal style of leadership which the Women's Union required.

The modest level of professional social work input from Rädda Barnen was also probably a significant factor in the Women's Union not succeeding to fulfil its promise. Interestingly, the school accepted and rose to the challenge to respond to the broader psycho–social needs of its pupils, but rather than uncritically accepting Rädda Barnen's concept of how this should be achieved, the teachers' group *developed their own approach*. In contrast to typical Western approaches, the school's strategy emphasised the *collective* nature both of the psychological problems being addressed and of the way in which they should be approached.

Good community work is based on a positive view of humanity: it sees refugees as being *resourceful, creative and committed* to the well–

being of their own community. It avoids the negative and cynical perception of refugees as passive, dependent and exploitative. The teachers demonstrated a natural understanding of psycho–social needs, an awareness of their own emotional needs, and a real desire to assist children who had been affected by their experiences. The school provided a situation in which they could use their own, largely intuitive understandings, and help to provide a range of ways in which, collectively, people could find ways of coping with these difficult experiences in a culturally appropriate manner.

References

Part 1

1. The concept of post-traumatic stress disorder was included in the American Psychiatric Association "Diagnostic and Statistical Manual lll (DSM lll) in 1980.

2. Case study: "From Clinic to Community": the Work of Acisam in El Salvador" on page 94 of this volume.

3. Case study: "Promoting Community Healing Networks: the Work of the National Children and Violence Trust", South Africa on page 126 of this volume.

4. Richman, Naomi (1993): "Annotation: Children in Situations of Political Violence", Journal of Child Psychiatry, Vol. 34, No. 8.

5. Concise Oxford Dictionary.

6. Anna Freud and Dorothy Burlingham (1943): "War and Children", NY, Medical War Books page 67.

7. Everett M. Ressler, Joanne Marie Tortorici and Alex Marcelino (1993): "Children in War: a Guide to the Provision of Services", New York, Unicef, page 174.

8. Patrick J. Bracken and Joan E Giller: "Responses to Trauma: Do Current Concepts Betray an Ethnocentric Bias?" mimeo.

9. Case study: "Promoting Community Healing Networks: the Work of the National Children and Violence Trust, South Africa" on page 126 of this volume.

10. Ibid.

11. This approach is outlined in the appendix to the case study.

12. Case study: "Timely Social Work Intervention in Refugee Emergencies: the Work of the Standby Team" on page 142 of this volume.

13. Alastair Ager (1994): "Mental Health Issues in Refugee Populations: a Review" - Working Paper of the Harvard Centre for the Study of Culture and Medicine, Harvard Medical School.

14. Case study: "Psycho-social Care for Children with Refugee Background: the work of Rädda Barnen's Swedish Department" on page 174 of this volume.

15. Case study: "Contamination by War: Strategies for Restoration by Collective Action" on page 190 of this volume.

16. Case study: "Building on Traditional Strengths: the Unaccompanied Refugee Children from South Sudan", on page 158 of this volume.

17. Dr. Friedrich Losel (1994): "Resilience in Childhood and Adolescence" in "Children Worldwide: the Family and Child Resilience", Geneva, ICCB.

18. Case study: "Contamination by War: Strategies for Restoration by Collective Action" on page 190 126 of this volume.

19. Margaret McCallin and Shirley Fozzard (1990): "The Impact of Traumatic Events on the Psychological Well-Being of Mozambican Refugee Women and Children", Geneva, ICCB.

20. Case study: "Contamination by war: Strategies for Restoration by Collective Action", on page 190 of this volume.

21. Case study: "Building on Traditional Strengths: the Unaccompanied Refugee Children from South Sudan", on page 158 of this volume.

22. Case study: "Promoting Community Healing Networks: the Work of the National Children and Violence Trust" – quoted from page 126 in this volume.

23. Katz, R. (1989): "Healing and Transformation: Perspectives on development, Education and Community" in White, Merry I. and Pollak S. eds (1986): "The Cultural Transition: Human Experience and Social Transformation in the Third World and Japan"; Boston, London and Henley, Routledge and Kegan Paul.

24. Case study: "Timely Social Work Intervention in Refugee Emergencies: the Work of the Standby Team" on page 190 of this volume.

25. Nicole Dagnino: "Responding to the Psychosocial Needs of Refugee Children: a Multifaceted Approach" in Margaret McCallin: "The Psychologial Well-Being of Refugee Children", Geneva, ICCB (1992), quoted from page 191.

26. Case study "Contamination by War: Strategies for Restoration by Collective Action" on page 190 of this volume.

27. Punamaki, RL (1992): "Natural Healing Processes and Experiences of Political Violence" - paper presented to the meeting on The Mental Health of Refugee Children Exposed to Violent Environments, Refugee Studies Programme, Oxford, January 1993 – cited in N. Richman (1993), Op. Cit

28. Case study "From Clinic to Community: the Work of Acisam in El Salvador" on page 94 of this volume.

29. Gerard Salole (1992): "Building on People's Strengths: the Case for Contextual Child Development", Bernard van Leer Foundation "Studies and Evaluation Papers" No 5, The Hague, Bernard van Leer Foundation.

30. Joanne Marie Tortorici: "Community Mental Health in Three Developing Countries: Nicaragua, El Salvador, South Africa" in Margaret McCallin (ed) (1992) Op. Cit, page 165.

31. Katz, R. and Wexler, A (1989): "Healing and Transformation: Lessons from

Indigenous People (Botswana)" in Peltser, K. and Ebigbo, P. (eds.): Clinical Psychology in Africa, Nigeria, Emugu, page 26.

32. Ibid page 36.

33. Ibid page 20.

34. Ibid page 21.'

35. Pamela Reynolds (1990): "Children of Tribulation: the Need to Heal and the Means to Heal War Trauma", "Africa" 60 (1), quoted from page 1.

36. Case study: "Promoting Community Healing Networks: the Work of the National Children and Violence Trust, South Africa on page 126 of this volume, page 4.

37. Case study: "Building on Traditional Strengths: the Unaccompanied Refugee Children from South Sudan" on page 158 of this volume.

38. Case study: "Contamination by War and Restoration by Collective Action" on page 190 of this volume.

39. James Garbarino, Kathleen Kostelny and Nancy Durbrow (1991): "No Place to be a Child", Toronto, Lexington Books.

40. B. Bettelheim (1943): "Individual and Mass Behaviour in Extreme Situations", Journal of Abnormal and Social Psychology, 38, page 417 - 452, cited in James Garbarino et al "Developmental Consequences of Living in Dangerous and Unstable Environments: the Situation of Refugee Children" in Margaret McCallin (ed) (1992), Op. Cit., page 15.

41. Jose-Luis Henriquez (1994): "Community-based Mental Health Projects for Persons Affected by the War and Former Child Soldiers in the FMLN" - in Rädda Barnen and Swedish Red Cross (1994) :"Child Soldiers", report from a seminar held by Rädda Barnen and Swedish Red Cross, Stockholm.

42. Ibid page 17

43. Anna Freud and Dorothy Burlingham (1943): "War and Children", New York, Medical War Books, page 67.

44. The preamble to the UN Convention on the Rights of the Child, 1989.

45. Nenad Rudić, Vida Rakić, Veronika Ispanović-Radojković, Svetomir Bojanin and Dragana Lazić (eds)(1993): "Refugee Children and Young People in Collective Accommodation" in Predrag Kalicanin, Jovan Bukelic, Veronika Ispanovic-Radojkovic and Dusica Lecic-Tosevski: "The Stresses of War", Belgrade, Institute for Mental Health. Quoted from page 87.

46. Case study "Contamination by War: Strategies for Restoration by Collective Action" on page 190 of this volume.

47. Elizabeth Ferris: "Refugee Women and Family Life" in Margaret McCallin (ed) (1992) Op. Cit.. Page 93

48. David Tolfree (1991): "Refugee Children in Malawi", London, ISCA, page 27f.

49. Case Study: "Timely Social Work Intervention in Refugee Emergencies: the Work of the Standby Team" on page 142 of this volume.

50. David Millwood (1995): "The Rädda Barnen Training Unit", Stockholm, Rädda Barnen, page 33.

51. This important issue is further discussed in Ulla Blomqvist (1995): "Community Participation in a Refugee Emergency – Focusing on Community Mobilisation, Women and Youth", Stockholm, Rädda Barnen.

52. Alistair Ager (1991): "Refugee and Community Mental Health and Children's Needs" in David Tolfree (1991): "Refugee Children in Malawi", London, ISCA.

53. Case Study "A Special Form of Social Interaction: the Work of Hi Neighbour in Yugoslavia" on page 109 of this volume.

54. Case Study "From Clinic to Community: the Work of Acisam in El Salvador" on page 94 of this volume.

55. The UN Convention on the Rights of the Child, Article 20.

56. Case study "Timely Social Work Intervention in Refugee Emergencies: the Work of the Standby Team" on page 142 of this volume

57. David Tolfree (1995): "Roofs and Roots: the Care of Separated Children in the Developing World", Aldershot, Arena. Lucy Bonnerjea (1994): "Family Tracing: A Good Practice Guide", London, Save the Children. Maggie Brown, Helen Charnley and Celia Petty (eds)(1995): "Children Separated by War: Family Tracing and Reunification", London, Save the Children. UNHCR (1994): "Refugee Children: Guidelines on Protection and Care, Geneva, UNHCR.

58. Case Study: "Timely Social Work Intervention in Refugee Emergencies: The Work of the Standby Team", on page 142 of this volume.

59. Case study: "Psycho-social Care for Children with Refugee Background: the Work of Rädda Barnen's Swedish Programme" on page 174 of this volume.

60. Article 3 of the UN Convention on the Rights of the Child, 1989.

61. Case Study: "Building on Traditional Strengths: the Unaccompanied Refugee Children from South Sudan", page 158.

62. David Tolfree (1995): "Roofs and Roots: the Care of Separated Children in the Developing World", Aldershot, Arena, Chapter 14.

63. Elizaeth Jareg (1987): "Psychosocial Factors in Relief Work during Famine and Rehabilitation", Oslo, Redd Barna, quoted in A. Ager (1994) op. cit.

64. Jan Williamson: "Mental Health Needs and Services for Refugee and Displaced Children" in Margaret McCallin Op. Cit. page 334.

65. Case study: "Timely Social Work Intervention in Refugee Emergencies – the Work of the Standby Team" on page 142 of this volume.

66. Case study: "Contamination by War: Strategies for Restoration by Collective Action" on page 190 of this volume.

67. Case study: "Promoting Community Healing Networks: the Work of the National Children and Violence Trust, South Africa" on page 126 of this volume.

68. Case study: "Psycho-social Care for Children with Refugee Background in Sweden: the Work of Rädda Barnen's Swedish Department" on page 174 of this volume.

69. Karin Edenhammar and Christina Wahlund: "No Development without Play!", Stockholm, Rädda Barnen, quoted from page 17.

70. Neil Boothby "Children of War: Survival as a Collective Act" in Margaret McCallin 1992 (ed) Op. Cit., quoted from page 171.

71. "Timely Social Work Intevention in Refugee Emergencies: the work of the Standby Team" on page 142 of this volume, page 9.

72. Case study: "Building on Traditional Strengths: the Unaccompanied Refugee Children from South Sudan" on page 158 of this volume.

73. Case study: "Building on Traditional Strengths: the Unaccompanied Children from South Sudan" on page 158 of this volume.

74. Case study: "Contamination by War: Strategies for Restoration by Collective Action" on page 190 of this volume.

75. David Tolfree (1991): "Refugee Children in Malawi", London, ISCA, P 38.

76. Case study: "Psycho-social Care for Children with Refugee Background: the Work of Rädda Barnen's Swedish Programme" on page 174 of this volume.

77. Case study: "Building on Traditional Strengths: the Unaccompanied Minors from South Sudan" on page 158 of this volume.

78. David Tolfree (1991): "Refugee Children in Malawi", London, ISCA.

79. Clare Hanbury: "Child-to-Child and Children in Camps". London, The Child-to-Child Trust.

80. Case study: "Promoting Community Healing Networks: the Work of the National Children and Violence Trust, South Africa" on page 126 of this volume.

81. Case study: "From Clinic to Community: the Work of Acisam in El Salvador" on page 94 of this volume.

82. Margaret Akello Kenyi (1995): "Emergency Teacher Training: the Case of South Sudan" – a paper presented to the International Conference on Education and Training for Refugees and displaced people, Makere University, Kampala, Uganda.

83. Naomi Richman, Eunice Mucache and Frieda Draisma (1991): "A School Programme for Helping War Affected Children" - Paper given at the Third Conference on Treating Victims of Organised Violence, Santiago, November 1991.

84. Case study: "Contamination by War: Strategies for Restoration by Collective Action" on page 190 of this volume.

85. Case study: "Building on Traditional Strengths: the Unaccompanied Refugee Children from South Sudan" on page 158 of this volume.

86. Jan Williamson, Op Cit page 331.

87. Gerald Caplan (1961): "An Aproach to Community Mental Health", London, Tavistock Publications.

88. Ibid page 4.

89. Case study: "Timely Social Work Intervention in Refugee Emergencies - the Work of the Standby Team" on page 142 of this volume.

90. Case study: "A Special Form of Social Interaction: the Work of Hi Neighbour in Yugoslavia" on page 109 of this volume.

91. Case study: "Building on Traditional Strengths: the Unaccompanied Refugee Children from South Sudan" on page 158 of this volume.

92. Case study: "From Clinic to Community: the Work of Acisam in El Salvador" on page 94 of this volume.

93. James Garbarino et al: "Developmental Copnsequeneces of Living in Dangerous and Unstable Environments: the Situation of Refugee Children in McCallin, M (ed) (1992) Op. Cit, page 13.

94. Case study: "Psycho-Social Care for Children with Refugee Background in Sweden: the Work of Rädda Barnen's Swedish Department" on page 174 of this volume.

95. Case study: "From Clinic to Community: the Work of Acisam in El Salvador" on page 94 of this volume.

96. Hlengiwe Mkhize (1992): "Children and Violence in South Africa" – Proceedings of the Workshop under the same name, Johannesburg, University of Witwatersrand.

97. Case study: "Promoting Comunity Healing Networks: the Work of the National Children and Violence Trust, South Africa" on page 126 of this volume.

98. Case study: "The Work of Acisam in El Salvador" on page 94 of this volume.

99. Naomi Richman, Eunice Mucache and Frieda Draisma (1991) Op. Cit.

100. Case study: "Promoting Community Healing Networks: the Work of the National Children and Violence Trust, South Africa" on page 126 of this volume.

101. Case study "Contamination by War: Strategies for Restoration by Collective Action", on page 190 of this volume.

102. Magne Raundalen and Rune Stuvland (1992): "The Child and Family in War", Stockholm, Rädda Barnen.

103. Case study: "From Clinic to Community: the Work of Acisam in El Salvador" on page 94 of this volume.

104. Ressler, E.M. Tortorici, J.M. and Marcelino, A (1993), Op. Cit. page 205.

105. Raundalen, M and Stuvland, R (1992), Op. Cit.

Part 11

[1] Loosely translated from Acisam (1993): "Strategic Plan Sketch, 1993 – 1995".

[2] The annual celebration is graphically recorded in an Acisam video: "The Third Anniversary of Ita Maura".

[3] Hi Neighbour is a not entirely satisfactory translation of of the Serbian "Zdravo da ste", a traditional form of greeting which is more accurately translated as "I wish you good health".

[4] Lev S. Vygotsky (1990): "Imagination and Creativity in Childhood". Soviet Psychology Vol 28 No. 1, page 87.

[5] Carole Wade and Carole Travis (1990): "Psychology", 2nd edition. New York, Harper Collins.

[6] UNHCR: Refugee Children: Guidelines on Protection and Care". Geneva, UNHCR 1994.

[7] See Rädda Barnen (1994): "Social Work in Emergencies: Capacity Building and Social Mobilisation – the Rwanda Experience", Stockholm, Rädda Brnen.

[8] David Tolfree (1991): "Refugee Children in Malawi", London, ISCA.

[9] This is also emphasised in Rädda Barnen (1995): "Protection of Children in Refugee Emergencies: the Importance of Early Social Work Intervention – the Rwanda Experience". Stockholm, Rädda Barnen.

[10] Quoted in Rädda Barnen: "Social Work in Refugee Emergencies: Capacity Builiding and Social Mobilisation – the Rwanda Experience". Stockholm, Rädda Barnen, 1994.

[11] The importance of this is highlighted Rädda Barnen (1995), Op. Cit, and in Rädda Barnen (1994): "Social Work in Refugee Emergencies: Capacity Building and Social Mobilisation – the Rwanda Experience. Stockholm, Rädda Barnen.

[12] UNHCR, Op. Cit.

[13] Rädda Barnen (1994): "The Unaccompanied Minors of Southern Sudan", Stockholm, Rädda Barnen.

[14] The term "children with refugee background" is preferred to "refugee children" as a means of emphasising that these are first and foremost ordinary children who happen to be refugees.

[15] The methodology used in this survey is set out in more detail in Eva Segerström (1994): "From Exposed to Involved", Stockholm, Rädda Barnen

[16] McCallin, M and Fozzard, S (1990): "The Impact of Traumatic Events on the Psychological Well–Being of Mozambican Women and Children", Geneva, ICCB.

[17] Ibid.

Abbreviations

FRY – Federal Republic of Yugoslavia
HIV – Human Immune Deficiency Virus
ICRC – International Committee of the Red Cross
IRC – International Rescue Committee
LWF – Lutheran World Federation
NCVT – National Children and Violence Trust
NGO – Non Governmental Organisation
OLS – Operation Lifeline Sudan
NY – New York
PTSD – Post Traumatic Stress Disorder
SCF (UK) – Save the Children (United Kingdom)
SPLM – Sudan People's Liberation Movement
STD – Sexually Transmitted Disease
UN – United Nations
UNESCO – United Nations Educational, Scientific
    and Cultural Organisation
UNHCR – United Nations High Commission
    for Refugees
UNICEF – United Nations Children's Fund
USA – United States of America